CLARA HARPER

MOM
INTERRUPTED

**THE 21-DAY MENTAL CLEANSE YOUR THERAPIST
WOULD PROBABLY NOT APPROVE OF**

Mom Interrupted:
The 21-Day Mental Cleanse Your Therapist Would Probably Not Approve Of
Copyright © Clara Harper 2025. All rights reserved.
Published by Published Nerd LLC
382 NE 191st St PMB 897079
Miami, Florida 33179-3899.

ISBN for Paperback: 978-1-966773-11-5
ISBN for Hardcover: 978-1-966773-12-2
First Edition: July, 2025
Printed in the USA

No part of this book may be used or reproduced in any manner whatsoever without written permission except in the case of brief quotations embodied in critical articles and reviews.
For information, address Published Nerd LLC.
www.ClaraHarperBooks.com
Published Nerd LLC

Dedication

For the moms who've reheated the same cup of coffee three times and still never finished it.

For the moms who've been peed on, cried on, yelled at, and needed a snack just as badly as the person screaming for one.

For the moms hiding in pantries, parked in driveways, and sitting on closed toilet lids just trying to feel something.

For the ones who are showing up anyway, even when their patience is gone, their hairdo is questionable, and their kids just told them they're "the meanest mom ever."

This book is for you.

You survived another day.
You're doing better than you think.
And even if you aren't?
You're still showing up.
That counts.
A lot.

Hello!

Welcome, Fellow Survivor.

If you're holding this workbook, odds are high that you've reached the mythical parenting phase known as "I'm fine, it's FINE," said through gritted teeth while stepping on something wet or sharp. You are a mom of littles. Which means you've wiped mystery substances off walls, negotiated with a child who refuses to wear clothes for philosophical reasons, and lost actual sleep over the question, "Was that poop?"

This is not a parenting manual. This is not a Pinterest-worthy growth chart. This is your emotional outlet, duct-taped together with caffeine and the sticky shit in the bottom of your purse.

You will not find peaceful affirmations here. You will not be asked to breathe through the chaos (unless it's through your mouth because something smells disgusting). What you will find here are full-page exercises to vent, laugh, cry-laugh, and check boxes you didn't know your soul needed. Think therapy... if therapy involved snot and booze.

This workbook was created for you, the chronically interrupted, the under-snacked, the I-didn't-know-their-shirt-was-backwards-until-lunch moms. The ones who have truly no more fucks to give and need a place to put it all.

So grab a pen. Lock yourself in the bathroom, and good luck.

Welcome to the book that won't ask you to improve anything.
Your motto for this journey: "If I can't fix it, I'll at least make fun of it... Maybe also while a little drunk." Now flip the page and begin your healing. Or at least passive-aggressive doodling.

Clara Harper

This book is...

A survival guide within a survival guide
So, you've cracked open this chaotic masterpiece. Congrats. That's step one. There's no wrong way to use this workbook, but there are ways to feel slightly more victorious while doing it. Here's the general idea:

Step 1: Pick a Day (Any Day)
You can go in order like a responsible adult, or flip to the page that screams, "THIS IS MY LIFE RIGHT NOW." There's no judgment here. This isn't a school assignment. It's emotional triage.

Step 2: Read the Intro
Each day starts with a real-life meltdown scenario pulled straight from the frontlines of motherhood, more specifically, my own life. Spoiler alert: you're not alone.

Step 3: *"Put it in the book"* -Regina
Check some boxes. Fill in the blanks. Doodle your rage. Journal. Name the unidentified stain. Think of this as your personal therapy session... only messier, louder, and with fewer co-pays.

Step 4: Do the Homework
At the bottom of each day, you'll be given a very specific task. Don't worry—it doesn't involve glue sticks or helping with math.
You'll know it when you see it. When that moment comes, stop everything and complete the assignment exactly as written. No skipping. No substitutions.
What is the homework? You'll find out on the next page.

Welcome to the workbook that doesn't ask you to be better, but instead accepts the feral.

ABOUT THE PROCESS

Look, motherhood isn't a sprint or a marathon. It's more like a chaotic obstacle course where someone keeps moving the finish line and throwing fruit snacks at your head. That's why this workbook isn't meant to be rushed or done in any particular order. Hell, do it in a sleep-deprived rage at 2 a.m. when you are soothing your baby.

Each day is a bite-sized dose of honesty, humor, and low-stakes reflection. It's here to help you notice the absurdity, find the funny, and maybe feel a little less like you're losing your mind. Take it step by step. Give yourself the five to ten minutes you deserve to finish each page. You don't need to have a breakthrough. You just need to show up, ideally with pants on, but honestly, we're flexible.

THE HOMEWORK

When the day has chewed you up, spat you out, and left you sticky, yelling, and slightly unhinged, that's when it's time to reward yourself. Look for the wine bottle symbol. That's your cue. Your sacred call to pause, breathe, and complete the "homework assignment" listed there.

Spoiler: the assignment is always a drink. You have survived another round of emotional dodgeball with tiny humans. No one else is going to give you a gold star for today, so consider this your official permission slip to treat yourself like the absolute legend that you are.

Intro Quiz
Are You Already Too Far Gone?

Check all that apply:

- ◯ You've said, "Don't lick that" in public.
- ◯ You've been handed something disgusting and told, "This is for you."
- ◯ You refer to your car as a mobile trash bin with seatbelts.
- ◯ You've stepped on something sharp, soft, or wet and decided not to investigate.
- ◯ You've said "Put your pants back on" more than once in a single morning.
- ◯ Your idea of self-care is sitting in the car alone with fast food and silence.
- ◯ You've googled "is ___ normal" and accepted that, in your house, it probably is.
- ◯ You've walked into a room and audibly asked, "Is that poop?"
- ◯ You've seen a child sprint naked through the house and just... let it happen.
- ◯ You've had to say the phrase, "We do not pee in that."
- ◯ You've looked around the room and thought, "Well, this is why I can't have nice things."
- ◯ You've considered leaving a mess where it is because tomorrow is future-you's problem.
- ◯ You told your kid to get their finger out of their butt more than 4 times in a single day.

Your Score:
Give yourself 1 point for every line checked, and 1 bonus point if you're currently hiding from your children.

Results:
0–1 points:
You might be new here. Enjoy your clean walls and your hopes. We'll see you again in three months, sleep-deprived and sticky.
2-4 points:
You've dipped a toe into the chaos. There's still time to escape, but you won't. You're emotionally bonded to a tiny wild roommate.
5-7 points:
Welcome to the fold. You speak fluent fart jokes and have accepted that someone is always yelling "MOM!" whether you respond or not.
8+ points:
You are one with the mess. A seasoned survivor. This workbook was made for you. Now flip the page, pour the coffee/wine/chocolate chips, and let's begin.

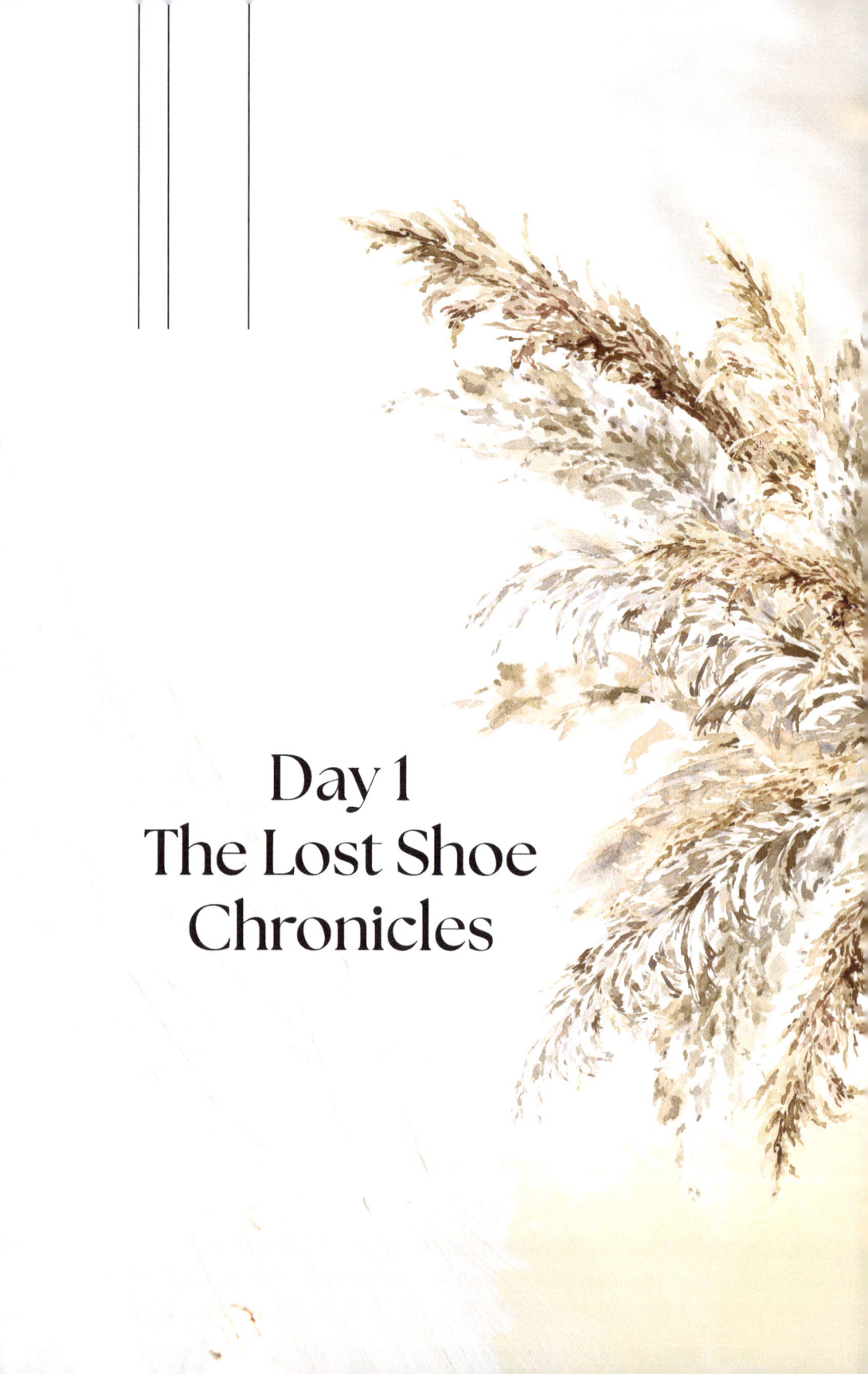

Day 1
The Lost Shoe Chronicles

If parenting had a national sport, it would be shoe hunting. I don't know what it is about children and footwear, but the moment you ask them to find their shoes, they lose the ability to visually process objects in space. My son once stood three inches from his sneakers—eye level, nothing in the way—and still shouted, "I can't find them!" with the confidence of a man absolutely sure he is being wronged.

It's like their brains short-circuit the second the words "go get your shoes" leave your mouth. And of course, this always happens when you're already running late, already sweating, already questioning every life decision that led you to this moment. That's when it happens: the gentle parent—the one who reads blogs and uses soft tones—slowly detaches from your body. She rises from your skin like steam off a scorched pot roast, floats silently toward the ceiling, and peaces out while you go deadpan and say coolly, "Try. Looking. Down. Right in front of you."

Mama, you are not alone. You are possessed by the ghost of who you used to be, and she is tired.
Maybe someday they'll find their own damn shoes, but it's not today. So we drink.

Let's have a soft introduction to what you can expect on the next pages. A simple check the box activity.

Where have you found your child's shoes? Check all that apply:
☐ Under the couch
☐ In the shower
☐ In the dog kennel
☐ Exactly where they should be but magically shrouded from your children's eyes

Expectation vs. Reality: The Gentle Parenting Spiral

I was going to be a gentle parent. I read the books. I followed the accounts. I practiced deep breaths and calming tones. I said things like, "I see you're having a hard time. I'm here when you're ready." I used phrases like "big feelings" and "kind hands." I narrated emotions like a toddler therapist. I truly believed that empathy could solve almost anything. Plot twist: I was locked in the bathroom crying before 9 o'clock every morning. Let's review what's real together.

EXPECTATION

- Use a calm, measured voice at all times
- Validate their feelings before offering solutions
- Get down to their level and make eye contact
- Say things like "use your words" and "you're safe"
- Model deep breathing during meltdowns
- Say "I won't let you hurt me" instead of "OW"
- Stay curious, not furious
- Avoid time-outs in favor of connection
- Narrate conflict resolution like Mr. Rogers
- End the day reflecting on how you peacefully parented

VS

REALITY

- Start with a calm voice, end with "WHAT THE FUCK DID I JUST SAY?"
- Validate your feelings with hidden junk food caches
- Eye contact replaced by side-eyes and winces
- Say things like "WHY are you like this" and "That's not food"
- Breathe deeply to stop yourself from throwing away every toy
- Say "I'm fine" while one eye is visibly twitching
- Stay furious, feel guilty, then repeat
- Time-outs now apply to you
- Narrate nothing because it's already chaos
- End the day scrolling your phone wondering if bedtime was too harsh or not harsh enough

Describe a time when your gentle-parenting soul ripped itself from your body, rendering you unable to act like a normal human being. Describe what caused it and how you responded to it.

Fill in the blanks:
The last time I saw both of my son's shoes together was _____.
The last time I found a shoe alone, it was in _____.

Fill in the bubble that matches your child's shoe status today:
○ Both shoes present and accounted for
○ One shoe MIA, presumed abducted by aliens
○ No shoes, just tantrums
○ Shoes worn on opposite feet, and no one noticed
○ Shoes found, but soaked, and no one knows why

How many times did you say "Where are your shoes?!" today?
0, 1-2, 3-4, 5+ (emergency)? _____

Describe where your shoes have "traveled" this week:
_____
_____
_____

Write a PSA to all missing shoes:
Dear shoes, please _____
so I don't lose my mind.

Reward yourself If you answered one email without a child interrupting you. First, how the hell did you do it? A Sommelier, please. Choose a *Provence-style Rosé* (light and dry) with notes of strawberry, watermelon, rose, herbs, citrus peel.

Pairs well with your mood because anything dry gives off an "I don't give a fuck" vibe. Let's face it, after today you don't have any left to give.

Day 2
The Laundry Apocalypse

Laundry isn't a chore anymore, it's a full-blown lifestyle. A slow, creeping villain that multiplies while you sleep and silently judges you. You haven't folded anything since last Tuesday, and at this point, the clean clothes live wherever they land. The socks have given up hope of ever being reunited and have likely unionized.

Their demands are unclear, but you suspect they involve better lighting and no more being shoved, unmatched, into the top drawer of your kid's dresser.

One day, your mother teaches you how to do laundry, and then— you do laundry every single day until you die. That's it. That's the legacy. You'll wash clothes no one remembers wearing. You'll fold the same shirt three times because no one puts it away. And don't forget the sacred ritual of rewashing the already clean clothes you left in the washer too long and now smell like a swamp. You know the smell. It haunts you.

In my house, we've stopped pretending. We now operate with three highly advanced **wardrobe systems**:
1. the floordrobe (clothes currently serving as carpet)
2. the basket wardrobe (clean-ish, probably, just dig)
3. the dryerdrobe (warm, ready, and located at the heart of our fashion philosophy)

Clothes now move through this elite loop: body → basket → washer → dryer → body. No folding. No drawers. No eye contact with the laundry pile.

Is it crazy? Obviously.
Is it sustainable? Surprisingly, yes.
Do I recommend it? With my whole heart.
So if you're out there drowning in piles, adopt the loop. And just know: you are not failing. You are functioning. You are laundry-looping like a champion. Now grab a glass of wine, toss that musty load back in (again), and remind yourself that wearing clothes fresh from the dryer is self-care.

Now, look at these calm photos and pretend for a moment that your life could be this calm and your house, this clean...

Check all that apply:
☐ One load in the washer for 3+ days
☐ Dryerdrobe level unlocked this week because folding is emotional labor
☐ Clean clothes still in baskets since last Tuesday
☐ Someone re-wore yesterday's clothes
☐ A mismatched sock colony is forming its own government
☐ You found a mystery stain on something
☐ You discover a particularly vile piece of dirty laundry mixed in a clean basket, and now you are sniff testing everything.

Write a 3-line warning to other women about the importance of not accepting laundry as your lifelong household chore:

_____
_____
_____

Fill in the bubble for everything that fits your laundry vibe today:
○ On top of it (for now)
○ Hanging by a thread
○ Just buy new clothes
○ Considering a nudist lifestyle

Number of socks found without matches today: _____

Create a new laundry detergent slogan: "Now with extra_____ for_____."

Confess the weirdest item you've ever laundered:
_____
_____
_____

Fill in the blanks: Current laundry backlog: _____ baskets, _____ piles of clothes on the floor, _____ regrets.

Fill in some more bubbles, because it feels good:
○○○○○○○○○○○○○○
○○○○○○○○○○○○○○
○○○○○○○○○○○○○○
○○○○○○○○○○○○○○
○○○○○○○○○○○○○○
○○○○○○○○○○○○○○

Write a poem below about where you washed, folded and put away the fucks you no longer have to give:

Treat yourself.

Reward Yourself with *Chardonnay*: Because You've Rewashed the Same Load Three Times This Week, and No One Gives a Fuck.

Chardonnay is a classic white wine known for its buttery finish, smooth vibe, and uncanny ability to pair perfectly with both grilled chicken and the slow unraveling of a woman who hasn't peed alone in six years.

Whether it's oaked, unoaked, poured aggressively into the closest glass, or just chugged from the bottle, it's here for you, especially on laundry day.

Because if you've sniff-tested a pair of pants like a crime scene investigator, discovered a balled-up wet towel that's now its own microbiome, or opened the dryer only to find the same load you forgot yesterday (and the day before), then congratulations. You're the reason Chardonnay exists.

It's creamy. It's comforting, and it totally counts as a reward for sorting, folding, and giving up halfway through. Best served cold, while you pretend folding is a meditative practice and not an endless, soul-draining loop of fabric and fury. But let's be realistic here, mama, you won't even get to finish it before it becomes lukewarm, just like this morning's coffee. It's OK though, because Chardonnay is still delicious at room temperature. Reward yourself with a glass, because in this house, the only thing getting pressed is wine grapes.

Day 3
Minivan Mayhem

Before we get started, look at this well-groomed, put-together woman who obviously doesn't have kids. Now put your laundry-day hoe-panties on and remember: you are still sexy.

You used to have a hot-girl car. Now you have a minivan. It used to be clean. It used to be functional. Even slightly scented. Now? It's a French-Fry-fueled biosphere, held together by car seats, sticky cupholders, and an ecosystem of forgotten snacks and emotional baggage. There's a layer of crumbs so thick it could support life, and you're pretty sure something under the passenger seat is fermenting.

And then you hear it—that slow, scratchy rrrrrrrip of Velcro—like nails on a chalkboard for moms everywhere. It's the unmistakable sound of your toddler taking his shoes off in the backseat...again. Because nothing says "car ride" like pulling into the parking lot only to realize your child is barefoot.

You used to enjoy driving. Now it's a rolling containment zone filled with empty juice boxes, sticky surfaces, and a faint but permanent smell of ketchup. You've accepted that your vehicle is now equal parts transportation device and mobile trash bin. You don't drive the car anymore—you negotiate with it. And if you've ever pulled into school pickup blasting the AC with a vent air freshener to cover the scent of rotting food and poop, you're not failing. You're parenting. And doing a damn good job at it, you magnificent bitch.

Vehicle Interior Inventory: What's Actually in There?
Check all that apply (no judgment, only solidarity):

☐ Crushed goldfish crackers embedded into a fabric surface
☐ An empty water bottle that rolls under your seat every time you brake
☐ A crumpled fast food napkin used as an emergency tissue
☐ A random sock (child-sized, unclaimed)
☐ Empty snack wrappers crumpled in a cupholder
☐ A dried-out baby wipe that somehow didn't clean anything and has a stain
☐ A clothing item someone "definitely" needed, then immediately discarded
☐ A school handout that's now overdue
☐ A plastic toy wedged so deep under the seat it's become part of the frame
☐ A crusty hair scrunchie stuck to the emergency brake
☐ A library book that was due over two weeks ago
☐ A banana peel you meant to throw out
☐ Furry french fries... Literally everywhere

Fill in the blanks: The strangest thing I've found in the car is _____.
Number of times I've turned around to yell today: _____

Fill in any or all bubbles describing your current car's condition:
○ Sort of clean if you squint
○ Lived-in chaos
○ Apocalyptic mess
○ Condemned zone

Finish this sentence: My car used to be _____, now it's _____.

Describe where that smell might be coming from:
(Artistic prompts: mold, poop, dirty clothes, farts, rotten milk in a cupholder out of reach) _____

Confess something you've never told anyone before about something you have done in your car. Tell us your dirty little minivan secrets:

_____
_____
_____
_____
_____
_____
_____
_____
_____
_____
_____
_____

Confessions of a Dirty Mom Car (Fill in the blanks)
At this point, it's basically a mobile landfill with car seats.

Today, I opened the back door and stared directly into a(n) _____ (adjective) war zone that smelled like _____ (food item) and _____ (bodily fluid). There were _____ (number) empty wrappers, a _____ (animal) sticker stuck to the ceiling rent free, and a _____ (random object) melted into the cupholder like a modern art installation.

I found a sock, no clue whose, a _____ (snack food) that might legally be a fossil, and a crusty _____ (candy or drink) that has chemically bonded to the upholstery.

I thought about cleaning it, but instead I muttered _____ (curse word), slammed the door shut, and drove off like nothing was wrong because that's how we cope now.

My car is no longer a vehicle. It's a _____ (dramatic nickname), a trash vortex with Bluetooth, and if one more mom side-eyes me in the school drop-off line, I will make direct eye contact while slowly deep-throating a gas station taquito like it's a power move.

Reward yourself today: with a *Pinot Grigio*: Because You Just Cleaned the Car with One Baby Wipe

Pinot Grigio is the clean, crisp white wine that says, "I see your cupholder full of melted fruit snacks and I support you anyway." It's light-bodied, mildly citrusy, and refreshingly indifferent to the fact that your backseat is currently a science project with a smell no one can identify. This is the wine for moms who have accepted that the "clean car" phase of life is over—and have instead embraced the art of brushing crumbs off the passenger seat like it's totally normal.

Tasting notes include:
– green apple
– lemon
– just a hint of "I don't get paid enough for this shit"

Best served chilled, preferably in a real glass.

Your car may be sticky, but your standards for peace and personal space don't have to be.

There's a list running in the background of your brain at all times. Milk, shoes, forms, the missing sock, emotional damage control, dinner ideas, that weird rash, snacks for tomorrow, guilt for yelling, and a vague feeling you're forgetting something really important. (You are, but you'll remember it at 2 AM.)

This is the mental load. It's heavy, it's invisible, and it never shuts up. Dump it all.

_____
_____
_____
_____

Day 4
What Did I Just Touch?
A Forensic Analysis

The incident began, as these cases often do, with a moment of hesitation. An innocuous graze against an unidentified surface while reaching between the cushions or beneath the car seat. The texture was ambiguous: somewhere between tacky and gelatinous, exhibiting a slow resistance to pressure and an unsettling elasticity that defied immediate classification. Suddenly, you are a scientific research analyst. Initial visual assessment was inconclusive; the substance bore no clear resemblance to any known food item within recent household inventory.

Olfactory analysis proved equally disconcerting. The scent was faintly sweet but carried an underlying note of decay, something once organic, now evolved into a new, unrecognizable phase of matter. Though the logical portion of the brain may insist it was merely jelly, possibly from a discarded sandwich, the auditory cue —the distinct squelch emitted upon removal—suggested otherwise. No reputable jam or preserve emits that level of emotional damage on contact.

It is in this moment, this tactile betrayal, that the parent is faced with a singular truth: children are capable of creating materials not yet documented by modern science. The consistency of regret. The scent of betrayal. The physical embodiment of "too late now."

Containment protocols are advised. Gloves, wet wipes, and emotional detachment are all recommended for future encounters. Proceed with caution. And never, under any circumstances, should you smell your fingers.

Use the Biohazard tracking calendar on the next page to document what you touched, smelled, or stepped in that defied logic and good hygiene. This is less about tracking soccer practice and more about understanding why your house smells like sour milk.

Each day, log the following:
Substance Description:
Examples: "Warm, sticky, and moving."
"Dry but suspicious."
"Could be jelly. Could be poop."

Sniff Test Result:
Chocolate
Not chocolate
Unknowable and traumatic

Emotional Fallout:
Gag reflex triggered
Audible gasp
Cried inside
Chose to forget

Optional Color-Coded Threat Level Key (fill in with markers or highlighters):
Green - Mild: Just yogurt or Play-Doh. Harmless. Probably...
Yellow - Concerning: Warm, tacky, and left a film
Red - Code Brown: Self-explanatory. Burn the evidence
Black - Do Not Investigate. It moved. It lives here now

"I reached into _____ and pulled out _____. My soul left my body."

Biohazard Tracker

Each time this month that you touch, smell, smear, or taste something questionable, document a short note here.

MONDAY	TUESDAY	WEDNESDAY	THURSDAY	FRIDAY	SATURDAY

Notes:

_____
_____
_____
_____

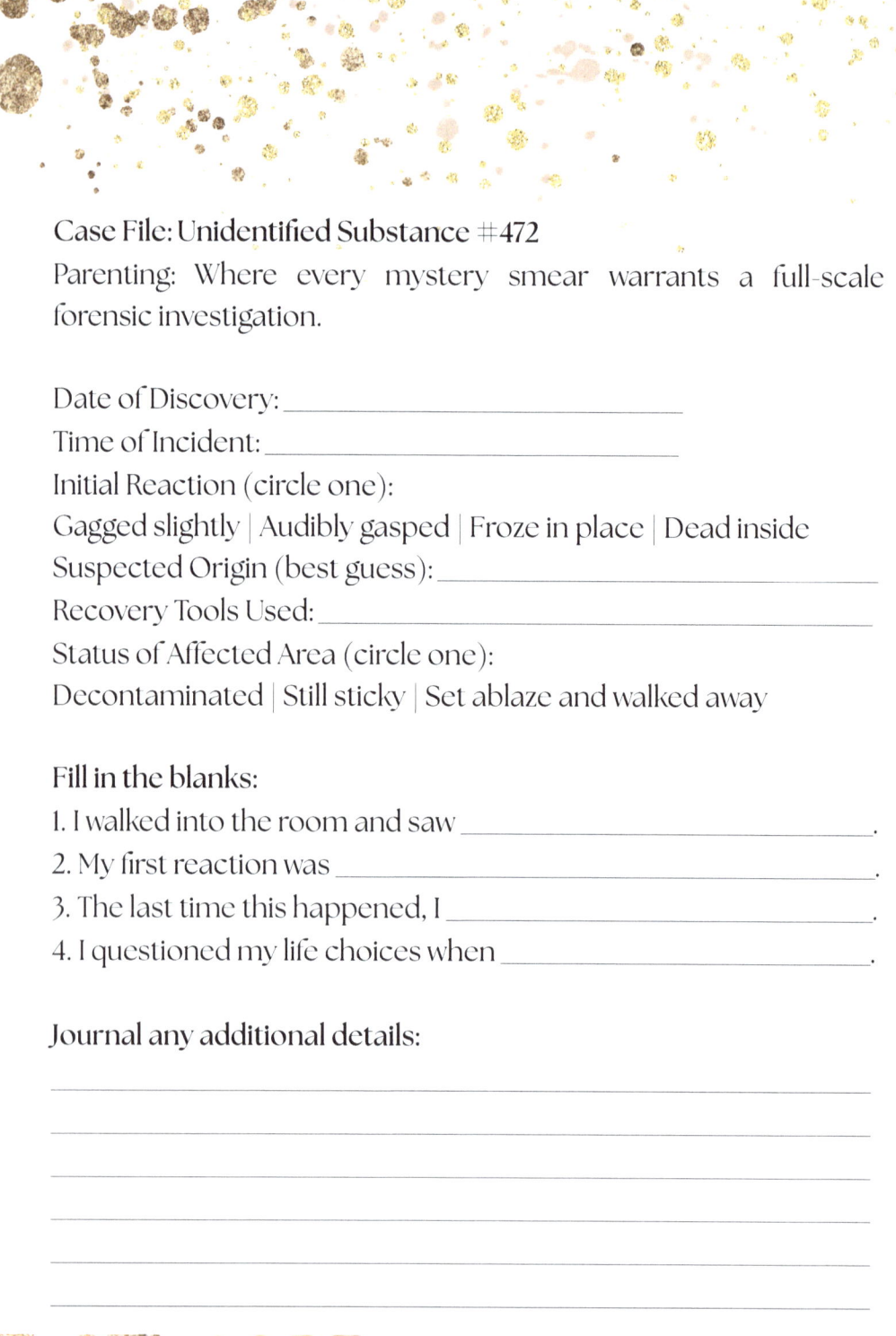

Case File: Unidentified Substance #472
Parenting: Where every mystery smear warrants a full-scale forensic investigation.

Date of Discovery: _____
Time of Incident: _____
Initial Reaction (circle one):
Gagged slightly | Audibly gasped | Froze in place | Dead inside
Suspected Origin (best guess): _____
Recovery Tools Used: _____
Status of Affected Area (circle one):
Decontaminated | Still sticky | Set ablaze and walked away

Fill in the blanks:
1. I walked into the room and saw _____.
2. My first reaction was _____.
3. The last time this happened, I _____.
4. I questioned my life choices when _____.

Journal any additional details:
_____
_____
_____
_____
_____

Scientific Method

OBSERVATION:
TODAY I TOUCHED

QUESTION: WHAT THE *WHAT* WAS THAT?

HYPOTHESIS:
IT FELT LIKE

EXPERIMENT:
I ATTEMPTED TO

DATA COLLECTION:
THE TEXTURE WAS

CONCLUSION:

I NOW FEAR:

Coping Strategy of the Day:
Circle One:
Deep Breathing | Hide in Bathroom | Call Another Mom | Bribe with Snacks | Give Up Gracefully

---

Reward yourself:
Riesling: Because You Just Touched Something That Might've Had a Pulse and Survived.

Riesling is the gentle, slightly sweet white wine that reminds you not all surprises are sticky and deeply upsetting. It has notes of peach, citrus, and emotional recovery, and it **pairs beautifully** with the psychological damage of pulling an unknown substance out of your couch cushions with your bare hand.

This is the wine for the mom who touched something moist, then panicked and grabbed the nearest napkin, only to have it shred immediately, leaving you holding the mystery substance with nothing but rising panic, and a strong desire to just set the couch on fire.

It's light, it's forgiving, and it doesn't judge the fact that you briefly considered just wiping it on your jeans and moving on.
Cheers, Mama!

Spill the tea: Confess here the most disgusting thing you or your kids have ever done. Don't hold back, Mama.

Day 5
Is that poop?

The true badge of parenthood isn't patience, sacrifice, or sleep deprivation—it's sniffing something mysterious and silently praying it's chocolate.

It starts with a startle reflex. You spot a smear on the wall, the couch, or, God help you, your own sleeve—and suddenly time stops. The room goes silent. The air thickens. The earth holds its breath with you.

Is it poop? Oh no. Tell me it's just remnants of yesterday's pudding cup. You are potentially mere seconds away from a moment so traumatic it'll be whispered about in your family group chat for years.

You don't blink. You don't breathe. You lean in and perform the sacred ritual of discovery: the sniff test, hoping for the sweet scent of cocoa and not the sharp sting of volatile compounds. Because nothing derails a Tuesday faster than mistaking poop for peanut butter.

And the worst part? No one else seems remotely concerned. Your child shrugs mid-mess: "I think it was from yesterday." Which somehow makes it worse.

Welcome to parenthood: where your detective skills peak in the bathroom, and your sense of smell becomes a frontline defense.

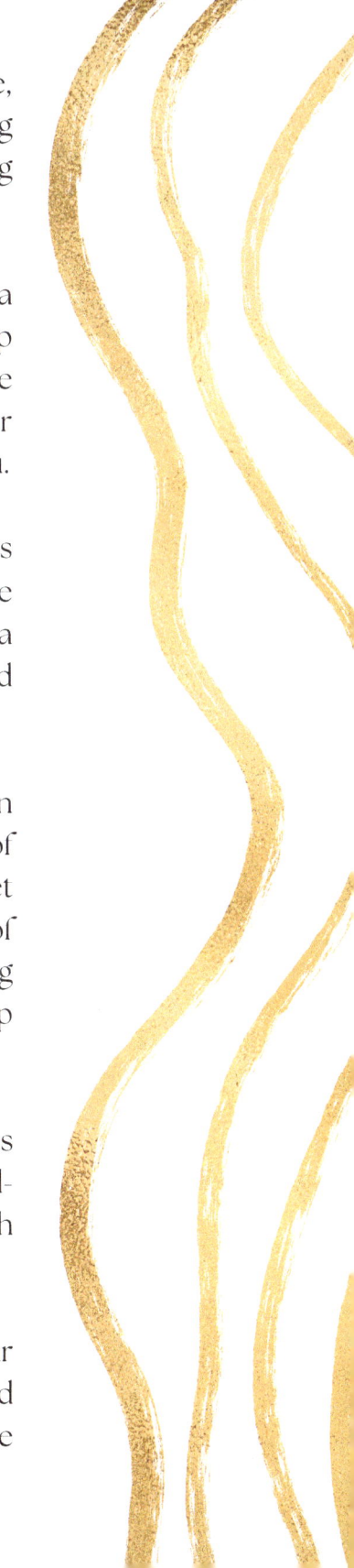

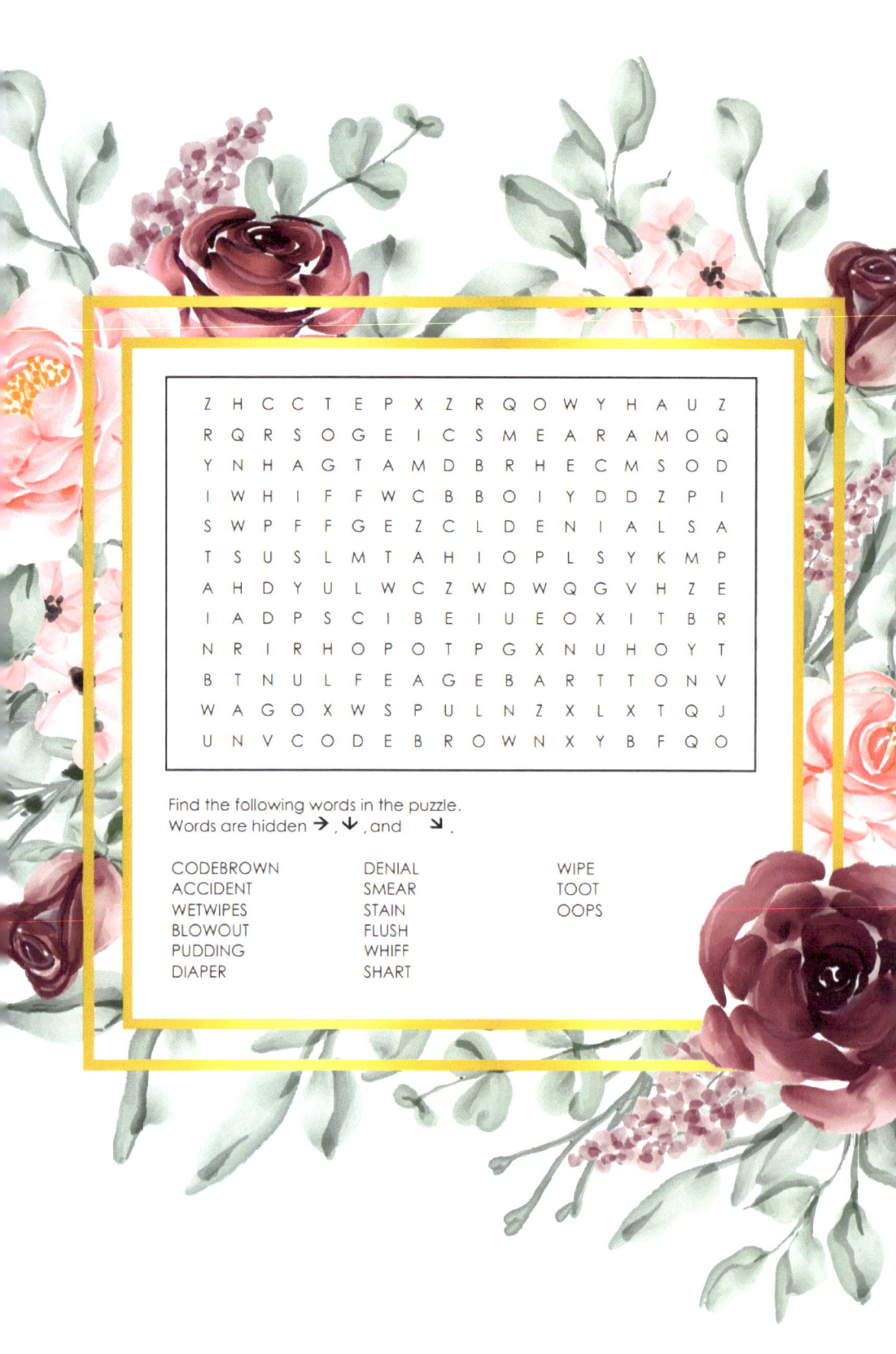

Fill in the blanks:

1. I walked into the room and saw _____.

2. My first reaction was _____.

3. The last time this happened, I _____.

4. I questioned my life choices when_____.

Check all that apply for today:
☐ Perform a taste test and immediately regret your life choices
☐ Declare a 'code brown' and summon backup with rubber gloves
☐ Pretend you saw nothing and walk away... slowly
☐ Panic-Google "what does raccoon poop look like?"
☐ Mentally relocate to a distant beach where things are clean and smell like coconuts

Write a haiku about a sniff test that ended badly:

_____
_____
_____
_____
_____

Self-care: Pour a glass of *Rosé*: Because You Handled a Code Brown Without Crying (*Much*)

Rosé is the pink-hued hero you didn't know you needed. Light, fruity, slightly dry, and most importantly—it pairs beautifully with emotional damage caused by a public blowout, a diaper failure of mythic proportions, or that one time you reached into your purse and pulled out a used wipe.

This is the wine for moms who've shouted "DON'T MOVE!" across a playground while holding a grocery bag like a hazmat kit. The ones who've experienced the trauma of poop under fingernails, or worse—the smell and subsequent search for mystery poop with no known origin.

Tasting notes include:
– strawberry
– melon
– the quiet triumph of surviving a day wearing white pants in the proximity of a potty-training toddler. Congratulations.

Best served cold, while you light a candle to mask the smell of shit. You've stared into the abyss (diaper), and you deserve something that sparkles.

Pour a second glass as a bonus if you managed to finish your lunch today while it was still hot. A third if you drank your coffee before it got cold.

Confess the most unspeakable thing you have experienced having to do with excrement or bodily fluids.

Day 6
Clutter Fatigue

It's not the mess you trip over. It's the mess you see. Constantly. That corner of the counter that's quietly growing an ecosystem of kid crap.

That end table that's turned into a "temporary holding zone" for important small objects you don't know what to do with (but feel weird throwing away).

The windowsill that has become a curated display of pinecones, googly eyes, a plastic ring from a cupcake, and a dry marker you keep thinking someone might revive.

It didn't happen overnight. It never does. It started with a rogue sticker sheet. A rogue action figure. A rogue rock. You didn't move them. And now that pile has a personality, and maybe a mortgage.

These aren't messes. They're clutter traps—and somehow, kids generate them like it's a biological function. Their pockets empty out into all four corners of your house like they're sprinkling breadcrumbs (and why is it always in the kitchen?!), and now there are six tiny cars "parked" on your microwave and rubber dinosaurs peeking out of the fruit bowl.

And don't even get me started on the random screws and mystery parts from who-even-knows-what that my husband adds to the pile, like he's building a robot no one asked for. This book is about motherhood, after all, but the impact of those piles is significant too. The piles are always "meaningful" to someone, and never urgent enough to deal with—until they multiply. Which they do. Daily.

Check all clutter zones currently thriving in your home:
- ☐ "To be sorted" pile of school papers that expired last semester
- ☐ A pile of rocks
- ☐ The spot on the stairs where everyone puts stuff "to take up later," and never, ever does.
- ☐ A shelf in the kitchen that's half pantry items, half kid's meal toys
- ☐ Toys left next to the sink because "they were giving them a bath"
- ☐ A stack of drawings labeled "For You, Mommy" that you feel too guilty to toss
- ☐ The shoe rack full of everything except shoes
- ☐ A bowl of rubber bands, Band-Aids, and hair ties you'll never use
- ☐ A "treasure" pile on a windowsill that no one will explain
- ☐ A plastic bin labeled "train track" that contains zero actual train related toys

Write Short Answers:
What's the most confusing object you've had in plain sight for over a week? _____

Which pile has emotionally worn you down the most?
_____

What item are you pretending is "sentimental" so you don't have to make a decision about it? _____

What's something on your counter right now that belongs in an entirely different room? _____

Creative Exercise: Give a title and museum-style description for the weirdest pile in your home:

Exhibit Title: "_____"
Curated By: A child with unclear intent

Materials: _____
Purpose: Unknown. Possibly sacred.

Reflection Moment: Complete this timeline for a pile in your home:

It started with: _____

I ignored it because: _____

Now it contains: _____

My current emotional relationship with it (fill in any or all bubbles):
○ Mild anxiety
○ Deep resentment
○ Stockholm syndrome
○ I leave the piles so I can feel something

Sweet. Bold. Full-bodied. Slightly unhinged. *Zinfandel* is the wine for the mom who has seven surfaces covered in "meaningful" objects, none of which spark joy, and all of which seem to multiply overnight.

Pairs well with:
– Craft scraps too weird to keep, too guilt-laden to toss
– The mental load of remembering who made what and whether it can go in the trash

Tonight, sip your wine while staring at one of your piles with a sense of calm indifference.
You're not cleaning it.
You're not sorting it.
You're simply coexisting.
And that's enough.

I'm thirsty for more tea. You may be drinking classier booze today than you used to BK (before kids), but confess here one of your less than classy escapades. Let's really go back into it, Mama. Tell this author about a time when you really went to the window, to the wall.

Day 7
The one about Toilets

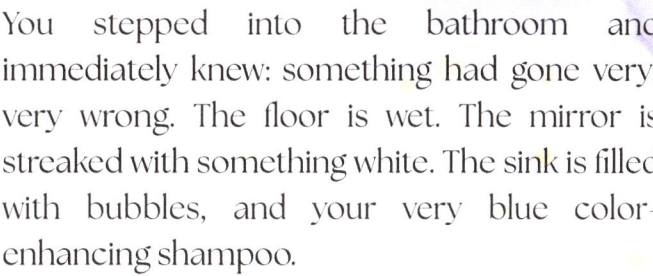

You stepped into the bathroom and immediately knew: something had gone very, very wrong. The floor is wet. The mirror is streaked with something white. The sink is filled with bubbles, and your very blue color-enhancing shampoo.

Somewhere in the corner, a toothbrush sticks out of the training toilet bowl.

At some point, possibly the minute you let your guard down, they decided that personal hygiene products were actually a junior chemistry set. Shampoo is now a magic potion. Toothpaste is paint. Soap? A slip-n-slide. The toilet paper roll has been unraveled and carefully draped over the towel rack "to dry it off," and from behind the shower curtain, someone is proudly announcing they've mixed lotion, hand soap, and mouthwash into a "cleaning potion" that they're now using on the tile grout. You don't remember signing them up for a STEM class. And yet, here you are.

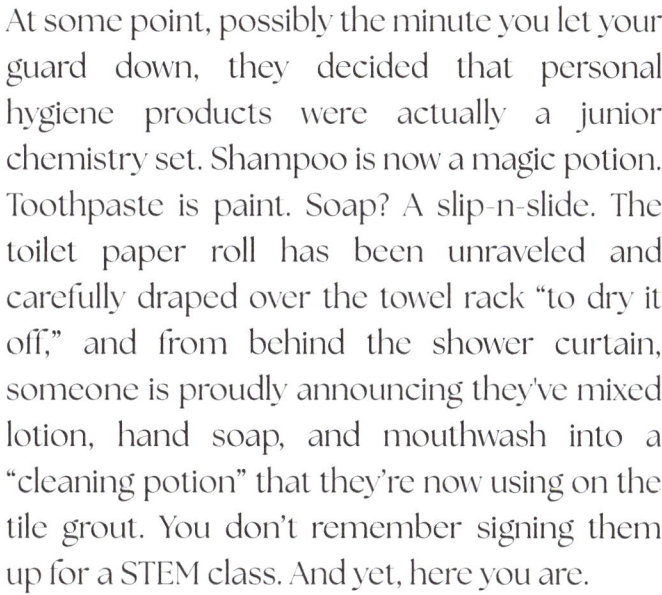

You quickly calculate in your head what kitchen utensil will fit in the toilet to get whatever toy you see, out. There's a faint scent of wet towel, bubblegum shampoo, and that musty, questionable smell that happens when water sits too long in a plastic toy

You just wanted one moment of peace. But the boys, *your husband's children*, had other plans.

Check all that apply:
- ☐ Plugged toilet because a child unraveled a roll of toilet paper into it
- ☐ Toothpaste mural
- ☐ Slipped on bubble bath suds
- ☐ Someone tried to flush a toy
- ☐ Your expensive shampoo or conditioner was used and abused
- ☐ Shaving cream explosion

Fill in the blanks:

Most baffling bathroom item used for "science": _____

My child mixed _____ (substance) with _____ (cleaning item) and called it "The Potion of _____ (absurd power)."

Science Activity: Write a short hypothesis for what they *thought* would happen.

_____
_____

Describe your current mental health status in three words:
_____

Take a deep breath (through your mouth—you don't know what that smell is), and use this exercise to shift your mindset from "I live in a nightmare" to "I live in a very wet, very loud art exhibit curated by tiny people, with sticky hands."

The goal here isn't to clean. It's to cope—by reframing the chaos as intentional, if slightly unhinged, creative expression.

Step 1: Label the Chaos

Your bathroom isn't a disaster—it's a gallery. A highly experimental, emotionally volatile gallery showcasing the unfiltered genius of preschool-aged artists working exclusively in household hygiene mediums.

Start by naming some of the standout works on display. Think Museum of Modern Art meets meltdown.

Examples:
- The smeared toothpaste on the mirror? "Whispers of Winter"
- A clump of hair + soap in the sink? "Texture Study in Drainage"
- Unraveled toilet paper wrapped around the towel rack? "Modern Fragility"
- Toothbrush in the training toilet? "Submission to Chaos, Vol. 2"

Now it's your turn.
List and name two "exhibits" discovered in your bathroom today:
  1a. Object or mess: _____
  1b. Title of the piece: "_____"
  2a. Object or mess: _____
  2b. Title of the piece: "_____"

Tonight's Reward: *Grenache*

Light enough to sip while scraping dried toothpaste off the mirror, bold enough to power you through convincing small humans that "helping clean up" does not mean pouring milk on the dog.

Grenache is playful, full of bright red fruit, and slightly spicy—kind of like your kids when they scream every time a drop of water touches their face.

Pairs well with:
  – The mysterious film now coating your sink
  – The toothbrush you just found soaking in the training potty
  – The moment your child said, "I cleaned up!" and you walked in to find shampoo finger paint on the cabinet under the sink

Drink it from a chipped mug you grabbed off the counter because every glass you own is suspiciously sticky. Besides, we all know the nice ones you got for your wedding were destroyed by the kids years ago.

You made it through the bathroom science fair, suds explosions, and a toddler declaring himself "Potion Master."

Here's to you. May your Grenache be juicy, your bathroom recover quickly, and your next "quiet moment" actually be quiet.

Odds are that you were today years old when you learned what a Grenache is. Use this space to write down your own signature drink recipe.

Day 8
Pocket Treasures

You were just trying to do laundry. That's it. Just a simple, responsible act of adulthood. You hear it before you see it. A sharp clank. Then a metallic thud, followed by a chaotic, irregular bang-bang-bang that makes your stomach drop. It's coming from the laundry room... Again.

You sprint in, already bracing for disaster, and there it is: your dryer, mid-cycle, throwing itself around like it's possessed. The sound is violent—like a toolbox in a tornado. You hit pause and crack the door open. Inside, everything is warm, damp, and traumatized.

There's a dozen socks, a half-dry hoodie wrapped in a fitted sheet like a laundry burrito, and lying there in the center—three fist-sized rocks.
Jagged. Filthy. Proud.
Pocket rocks... of course.

Your son's "very special treasures" have been through a full-speed spin cycle turned rock tumbler and now look somehow shinier and more determined to ruin your budget. The inside of the drum is visibly dented. One of the fins is cracked. And there's a long, fresh scratch down the back wall.

This is your life now: every load of laundry is now a high-stakes gamble with an emotional payoff somewhere between confusion and mild panic. You're not doing chores, you're a research assistant working on an archeological dig site. At this point, you're not sure if you're a mom or a one-woman lost-and-found department with a minor in ancient debris excavation.

Now you have a dead dryer and a weekend date with the appliance store, wild toddlers in tow. This should be fun. This week we need more than wine.

What pocket loot did you find this week? (Check all that apply):
☐ Rocks
☐ Unwrapped candy
☐ Something soggy
☐ Any variant of what your kid would call a stick
☐ A piece of sharp plastic or glass
☐ Crumbs from a snack that was "definitely saved for later"
☐ Writing utensil like a pen or crayon
☐ A dead bug

Fill in the blank:
The weirdest thing I've ever washed on accident:
_____
Then, describe how it looked when the load was done:
_____

Number of times I've said "EMPTY YOUR POCKETS" this week: _____ and the number of times they actually complied _____.

Item I considered keeping because honestly it was kind of cute:
_____

Pocket Poem
Make this one more interesting:
Roses are red, pockets are wild,
Today I found _____,
I questioned my life, then smiled.
Because let's be real—
What's a little _____ between friends,
When laundry never, ever ends?

Now, write your own Pocket Poem:
Write a 3-line poem titled: "Ode to the Pocket That Betrayed Me."
 Line 1: Describe the feeling when you reached in
 Line 2: What you found
 Line 3: Your emotional state afterward

_____
_____
_____
_____
_____

Across

2. Mysterious pocket object that short-circuited your sense of peace
3. Surprise! This "treasure" just cracked your dryer fin
4. What you found fused to the dryer drum that will outlive us all
6. Four months old, unreadable, still in every tiny pocket
8. Somehow ended up in the washer and now you need one to fix it

Down

1. Found on every surface, including the inside of the washer lid
3. What you had to do after your child used the dryer as a rock tumbler
5. Rolled out mid-cycle and made your appliance sound haunted
7. What turned the entire laundry pink and lemon-scented
9. Melted into fabric, possibly still edible according to your child

Answers on the next page!

For the money you're about to shell out on a new dryer—thanks to the backyard geology project in your kid's pockets—tonight calls for *Whiskey*. On the rocks, of course.

Sip it slowly, from your favorite glass, while you stare into the busted drum and wonder how many stones it takes to wreck an appliance built for adult life but not parenthood.

Pairs perfectly with:
  – A pile of damp clothes you're now drying with a hairdryer
  – A child explaining that the rocks were "for science"
  – The deep spiritual acceptance that this is your life now

Congratulations. You're 60% sommelier, 40% rock museum curator, and 100% still not throwing those jeans away.

Personally, this author takes her whiskey neat

Across:
2. BATTERY
3. ROCK
4. GUM
6. RECEIPT
8. WRENCH

Down:
1. STICKER
3. REPAIR
5. MARBLE
7. CRAYON
9. CANDY

Day 9
Messy Room Disaster Relief Plan

Welcome to the place where your tidy-home aspirations come to meet their noisy, sticky, battery-powered fate. Picture the scene: sunlight filters through the curtains, lands squarely on a glittering carpet of marbles, action figures, and Play-Doh crumbs that have been committed to a life sentence inside the fibers.

Somewhere beneath the rubble you suspect a floor still exists, though current evidence is thin. You pause, coffee in hand, contemplating whether to call in a professional cleaning crew or perhaps a priest for an exorcist.

Take a deep breath. You have stepped into a living museum of last year's birthday gifts, half-finished craft projects, and sentimental trinkets that nobody actually remembers receiving. Listen closely and you will hear the distant buzz of a toy drone that vanished weeks ago, forever circling the upper shelf like a plastic ghost. By the door lies a single sock filled with puzzle pieces, proof that even laundry is not safe from the uprising. The toy bins are overflowing, the shelves are visibly sagging, and the air smells faintly of apple juice and musty clothes.

Yet here you stand, noble parent, armed with Febreze, Nitryl gloves, and the promise of wine. Today we do not strive for perfection; we simply aim to carve out a navigable path from the doorway to the window, rescuing any valuable floor space we can claim along the way. Ready? Grab your hazmat gloves and your sense of humor.

Tick each box for emotional closure or future bragging rights:
- ☐ Sticky toy nobody claims
- ☐ Graveyard of Happy Meal toys
- ☐ Book pages tastefully removed by a toddler
- ☐ Puzzle with exactly 999 of 1000 pieces
- ☐ Toy-kitchen food that contains very real food crumbs
- ☐ Train track that loops straight into existential despair
- ☐ A toy you were certain you donated three months ago
- ☐ That one singing toy you thought ran out of batteries but now repeats partial sounds like it's possessed
- ☐ A ball, car, or figure wedged so deeply under the couch it qualifies as structural support
- ☐ Slime. Why is there always slime?

Fill in the blanks:
- The most cursed toy in this house is _____.
- If I hear the sound _____ one more time, I might legally change my name and disappear.
- My child once cried for three hours because I touched _____, which has been broken since 2019.
- I threw away _____ today and immediately hid the evidence. I regret nothing.

"Toy Emergency"

This morning, I stepped on a(n) _____ (adjective) _____ (object), screamed like _____ (celebrity), and then tripped over a _____ (animal)-shaped toy filled with _____ (gross substance).

I spent the next hour negotiating with my child about whether we could donate _____ (ridiculous number) toys, and we compromised by keeping _____ (equally ridiculous number).

If you found at least one item that:
☐ You don't recognize and are scared to touch
☐ Was instantly claimed as "super important" when you tried to throw it out
☐ Might be food... but also might not
☐ Is staring at you for some reason

Congratulations! You officially qualify for emergency wine distribution.

The rules state you receive a generous glass of wine and a guilt-free evening, because that room did not clean itself and you are still standing. Tonight's Pairing: *Pinot Noir*. Smooth, deep, and slightly dramatic. Just like your performance when pretending you didn't just rage-throw a toy into the trash five minutes ago.

Sip it slowly while staring at the clutter and wondering how your child owns more plastic fruit than real fruit.

Day 10
What Personal Space?

Remember personal space? No? That's fair. It's been missing since your child figured out how to breastfeed—and then when they could crawl, they decided their favorite place was directly behind you at all times, preferably while you're carrying hot coffee or trying to open a cabinet.

At this point, you are never alone. Not in the bathroom. Not in bed. Not even in your own brain. You can't change clothes without an audience. You can't text without your phone being snatched. You can't sit down without being climbed like Everest.

You are a pillow, a jungle gym, a 24/7 emotional support human. You've had your face squished mid-sentence, been followed into every room, and heard the shrill "*Mama!*" every single time you've dared to move toward the door—even if it's just to throw away a used tissue.

Your child is magnetic, and you are the metal. You are now legally required to provide commentary on all bodily functions, snacks, and outrageous scientific theories, even when you're just trying to go pee or stare blankly into the fridge for a second of quiet, and the worst part is that you can't do anything to stop it because the moment you tell a child to never do something is the moment they 'never' like they've never, nevered before.

IYKYK...

Let's document the invasion of personal space. For science.

All invasions of your personal space that occurred this week:
- Bathroom entry mid-wipe
- Asked you to stop looking at them while you were in the bathroom pooping
- Smashed your teeth throwing their head back at random while sitting in your lap
- "Surprise" lap landing while holding a full cup of coffee
- Nose pressed directly into your cheek while talking
- Sneezed in your mouth
- Climbed on you like a jungle gym while you were sleeping
- Used your body as a table, tissue, or trampoline
- Pulled your shirt down, publicly exposing a boob
- Full commentary while you were changing clothes (<u>bonus</u> if they put their finger in your buttcrack while you bend over)
- Crawled into your lap while you were pooping
- Painfully pushed off of your boob with their elbow to get up
- Whispered "Mom?" with their nose touching your eyeball

Fill in the blanks:

The last time I had privacy was
_____.

My child entered the bathroom to ask me
_____.

I knew I'd lost ownership of my own body when
_____.

The strangest place I've found a child curled up on me was
_____.

Automatic Thought Exercise:
"If one more person touches me, I will evaporate."
Now re-frame it:
"I am magnetic because I am safe, loved, and very warm. Also maybe I smell like snacks. That's fine."

Write your version:
My automatic thought: "_____"
A more helpful thought: "_____"
Now, remember that even if you spend hours "re-framing" reality with cognitive therapy, your kids will be just as clingy as they ever were. This is your life now and there is no physical escape. But alcohol is always there for you.

Enter, *The Cling-on-Free Cosmo*.
Because your body has not belonged to you since childbirth, and your child just tried to crawl into your shirt during a Zoom call.
Ingredients:
– 1.5 oz vodka (you earned it)
– 1 oz cranberry juice (because your kid just asked what color blood is)
– 1 oz triple sec (and .5 oz more for every time you've been climbed today)
– 0.5 oz lime juice (representing the sour scream of "MOOOM!" echoing down the hall)
Instructions:
Shake with ice. Strain into a fancy glass you never get to use. Sip in the hallway on the way to the only room with a lockable door while pretending you're invisible.
Pairs well with:
– The closet where you are hiding
– A smutty novel so unhinged that you'll need counseling

Day 11
The One Where You Let Them Dress Themselves

It started as an act of independence. "Sure, buddy, go ahead and pick out your pants." You were feeling optimistic. Maybe even a little proud. You thought, He's growing up.

Then he chose a pair of swim trunks from last July. It's 30 degrees outside. It's also picture day.

You stared for a few seconds, evaluating your options. You could fight it. You could wrestle him into jeans and a sweatshirt. But you know that having kids is all fun and games until you pick out the wrong pants, and then your day is over. You already saw your entire life flash before your eyes in slow motion during those two seconds when his t-shirt got stuck on his head.

So... you let it go and save your energy for the next battle. Because sometimes, fashion is not your hill to die on. It's the hill you quietly back away from while praying and holding out a snack like it's a "distraction steak" before a prowling lion.

He will strut out the door like he invented clothing. Confident. Proud. Like he is headed to a red carpet event.

Today's outfit was brought to you by chaos, confidence, and a complete lack of ability to choose proper pants, and honestly you kind of respect it. More importantly, if this was you today, you avoided another meltdown. I love that for you.

Check off what your child wore today:
- ☐ Pajamas as outerwear
- ☐ Shorts in cold weather
- ☐ Halloween costume
- ☐ Backwards or inside out clothing
- ☐ Nothing matched but confidence was high

Fill in the blanks:
The weather was _____, and he wore _____.
He said he picked the outfit because _____. That mom we hate (PTA Susan) commented that my son looked _____.

Calming exercise
Instructions: Check each box once complete. Bonus calm points if you didn't mutter "I give up" out loud.

- ☐ Step 1: *Inhale* slowly through your nose while silently repeating: "This is not the hill to die on. Sometimes my kid is just a cunt."
- ☐ Step 2: *Hold your breath* for four seconds while imagining yourself floating above the shitshow like a balloon—one that pays the bills on time, signs the permission slips, and gracefully rises above PTA-Susan's color-coded bullshit and her performative gluten-free cupcakes.
- ☐ Step 3: *Exhale* loudly through your mouth like you're blowing away the judgment of school drop-off moms in full hair and makeup while they look your bathrobe and slippers up and down.
- ☐ Step 4: *Repeat* this cycle until one of the following happens:
  – Your blood pressure drops
  – You stop caring what anyone thinks
  – Your child adds something weirder to the outfit and you reach emotional numbness

Write your outfit red carpet commentary for the day: "Today, my child _____

_____."

Fill in the bubble for your fashion strategy:
○ Insist on appropriate clothes
○ Let it go - Natural consequences are educational
○ Add layers when he's not looking
○ Take photos for future blackmail

While you are at it, fill in all of these bubbles, (bonus for using different colored pens):
○○○○○○○○○○○○○○○○○○○○○○○○○○○
○○○○○○○○○○○○○○○○○○○○○○○○○○○
○○○○○○○○○○○○○○○○○○○○○○○○○○○

Reward your new and calmer self: *Merlot* is smooth, medium-bodied, and forgiving—kind of like the attitude you aspired to have this morning when your child came downstairs dressed like an idiot.

This is the wine for the mom who glanced at her child's outfit, took a long breath, and said, "Looks great, bud," because picking a fight over pants was not in today's emotional budget.
Tasting notes include:
– black cherry
– plum
– faint hints of "fuck-off, PTA Susan!"

Best enjoyed in a quiet room alone, ideally after the fourth stranger complimented your child's "creative spirit" while you explained, once again to your kid, that it wasn't Halloween.

Day 12
Bathtime Battlefield

Bath time was supposed to be the calm after the storm. You'd finally reached the finish line after making a healthy dinner, serving it to your ungrateful children who wouldn't eat, and snuck away from the table like a seasoned escape artist, leaving your husband with the mess and the noise while you began your mission to "get the bath ready." Translation: ten minutes of breathing in solitude while using the removable showerhead to aggressively create bubbles in the tub like it's a critical task only you can manage. The water had just started filling and maybe—just maybe—you'd carved out one sliver of temporary peace.

But of course, they followed you. Not one minute later, you heard the thundering footsteps. The door creaked open. One was already undressing, the other was singing some kind of bath battle chant and tossing toys in the tub like depth charges. So much for the peaceful transition to bath time.

Within seconds, someone shouted about the water being too hot. You tried to wash hair without triggering a full meltdown. You failed. Someone started yelling about soap in their eyes (preemptively, before any actually got there), and the next thing you knew, you were soaked from the knees down while holding a bottle of shampoo like a white flag. The soap always creates traumatic drama, even though it is labeled "tear-free".

The bathroom floor? A disaster zone. All nearby towels? Soaked. The walls? Suspiciously splattered. No one is clean, and bedtime feels further away than ever.

Tonight's parenting lesson: *Bath time is not a wind-down ritual.* It's a high-stakes aquatic negotiation with tiny people who think rinsing is optional. Reward suggestion? Something stronger than bubble bath. Probably in a glass. Maybe behind a locked door.

Check all that apply to tonight's bath:
- ☐ Someone screamed "TOO HOT!" while testing the water with their foot for 0.052 seconds
- ☐ Suddenly hated bubbles (after demanding bubbles)
- ☐ Asked for one toy, then cried about that toy
- ☐ The toddler pooped in the tub. Again.
- ☐ Screamed like a banshee during hair rinsing
- ☐ Escaped mid-bath and ran down the hall wet and naked
- ☐ Slapped sibling with a soaked washcloth
- ☐ "Accidentally" drank the bathwater
- ☐ Used shampoo to fingerpaint the wall

Fill in the blanks:
The bath started out _____, and ended _____.
If I could assign a bath time soundtrack it would be sung to _____.

Bubble bath Math:
Soap used: _____ pumps
Time spent rinsing screaming children: _____ minutes
Times I considered abandoning ship mid-wash: _____
Number of towels used to dry one (1) child: _____
Number of towels used to mop up the floor: _____

Cognitive Therapy Reframe:

Default thought: "I swear to God if they splash water one more time..."

Reframe it:
"I am not drowning—I am being cleansed by the tears of my own maternal patience."

Write yours:
My automatic thought: "_____"
My upgraded survival mantra: "_____"

Wine Reward: *The Bathtime Breakdown Cabernet*
Because you just wrestled two slippery goblins into a tub, dodged shampoo like it was acid, and somehow ended up wetter than both of them.

Pairs perfectly with:
– Your soaked bra
– A trail of tiny wet footprints
– The quiet sound of your will to live circling the drain
– Giving zero fucks

Tasting notes:
– Deep, dark fruit with undertones of regret
– Bold, full-bodied—like your toddler's refusal to rinse
– Finishes with a dry snap of "I said SIT DOWN IN THE WATER" energy

Day 13
Kitchen Catastrophe

It started, like most of your worst decisions, with good intentions. You were trying to be a "fun mom." The kind of mom who makes pancakes or muffins or something wholesome on a slow afternoon instead of shoving dry cereal at the children and whispering "please stop touching me" into a coffee cup.

"Can I help?" they asked. You paused. You knew better. But a small, stupid part of you thought, maybe this time will be different. Maybe this time, you'll be the kind of mom who bakes with her kids in matching aprons, giggling as clouds of flour float through sunbeams like a charming Pinterest video come to life. Instead? Chaos. Immediate, sticky, flour-in-your-bra chaos.

One child began licking the cinnamon container like it was a push-pop. The other child sneezed directly into the batter. Eggshells made it in, of course—because apparently, cracking an egg with your whole fist is a sensory requirement now. Someone cried because mom said they couldn't hold the mixer. Someone else cried because they weren't crying yet and didn't want to feel left out.

There are three open spice containers—none of them the right one—and one suspicious puddle on the floor that may be melted butter *or urine*, and frankly, you don't have the bandwidth to investigate.

You are now sticky, salty, vaguely vanilla-scented, and three seconds away from crying into a produce bag. You stare at the mess, open a cabinet, pull out the box cereal, and whisper: "Dinner's ready."

This page isn't about what they did. This is about you.
Specifically, how many *questionable* behaviors you exhibited while pretending to "stay calm" during your child's culinary crime debut.

For each scenario, check: Red Flag, Normal, or Both. *Red Flag*: Unhinged; *Normal*: your mother might approve, *Both*: I think you understand...

You screamed "EVERYONE OUT!" More than once.
☐ Red Flag ☐ Normal ☐ Both

You poured yourself a second full glass of wine at 3:13 p.m.
☐ Red Flag ☐ Normal ☐ Both

You licked frosting off your finger and immediately followed it with a whispered "fuck this" and went back for more.
☐ Red Flag ☐ Normal ☐ Both

Your child said, "Are you okay?" and you said, "I could use a cigarette."
☐ Red Flag ☐ Normal ☐ Both

You threatened to send kids to bed without dinner.
☐ Red Flag ☐ Normal ☐ Both

You made your toddler the Sous Chef and blamed them for everything that went wrong.
☐ Red Flag ☐ Normal ☐ Both

You ate a raw cookie dough in your pantry, in the dark with your back to the family like a goblin.
☐ Red Flag ☐ Normal ☐ Both

You told Alexa to play "R-Kelly," and let your kids dance to songs about pimps and hoes.
☐ Red Flag ☐ Normal ☐ Both

You screamed at the stand mixer, cried, then aggressively cleaned it like it had wronged you personally.
☐ Red Flag ☐ Normal ☐ Both

You fed everyone cereal for dinner because you were simply fucking done.
☐ Red Flag ☐ Normal ☐ Both

Day [_____]: If This, Then That – Kitchen Chaos Edition

You invited a child into your kitchen. They offered to help. You said yes. The timeline is now broken…

Let's chart your emotional descent and see if you made it out alive. Circle each option you go with. We aren't looking for a right answer, this is simply *the therapy process*. There will be alcohol later so just roll with it and stop asking so many questions.

START HERE
Did they offer to help or just show up with sticky hands?
→ Offered → You said yes. Like a dumbass. Continue.
→ Showed up → Too late. They're already involved. Continue.

Was something dropped, smeared, or dumped in the first 2 minutes?
→ Yes →
→ Did you clean it?
→ Yes → With an actual towel? Or your shirt sleeve?
→ No → "It adds flavor." Move on.
→ No → They're plotting something worse. Stay alert.

They touched something and then touched something else.
→ Hands went from hair → food? Kick them out and order takeout.
→ Hands went from floor → face → back in the bowl? STOP and serve cereal.
→ All of the above? → Accept your fate. Continue.

They asked to stir something.
→ You handed them the bowl.
→ They immediately flung it like a discus.
→ You said, "Great job, bud!" while suppressing a scream. Continue.

Did they make up a new "recipe"?
  → You asked what it was for.
  → They said "It's for dogs / witches / a potion / my mouth."
  → You asked no further questions. Continue.

You gave them a job. Did it end in:
Broken utensil?
Loud crash?
Someone yelling "It's fine!" before you even said anything?
  → Yes → Continue
  → No → Either you're lying or this is your first child. Continue.

They said "Oops."
  → Immediate fight-or-flight response.
  → You made eye contact with the mess.
  → You considered leaving. You didn't.
  → You made a sound only other moms can hear. Continue.

Did they "accidentally" eat something they weren't supposed to?
  → You Googled "Can kids eat that" with one hand while pretending it was fine with your face.
  → No one vomited. You win. Continue.

Final Outcome: Was something technically "made"?
  → Yes → It is... edible-adjacent. Applaud them and serve cereal.
  → No → Blame the oven. Blame the recipe. Blame society.

End Result, If you:
□ Didn't cry
□ Didn't threaten to move out
□ Still love your child (even a little)
Get the cocktail shaker out. Its 5-oclock somewhere.

You earned this. Not because you cooked. Not because anyone ate it. But because you let a tiny, overconfident person with zero hygiene standards operate a hand mixer unsupervised—and you're still standing.

Vermentino is a crisp, dry white wine that says:

"I saw what happened here and I still love you. But also… what the fuck?"

Tasting notes include:
- Lemon peel
- Sea breeze
- A faint whisper of "How did *that* splatter on the ceiling?"

Best served in the cleanest cup you can find (read: sippy with no lid)
While hiding behind the fridge door, fake-crying into shredded cheese as you declare, "Dinner is canceled."

Pairs beautifully with:
Questionable batter on your shirt A broken spatula in the trash. And the moment you pretend not to hear them say, "I want to help again tomorrow."

Pour yourself a glass, a big one.
You made memories today.

Day 14
Beware the Silence

It was suspicious from the beginning. You noticed the quiet—but instead of acting on it, you let yourself believe the lie. "They're probably just playing."
"Maybe they're tired."
"Maybe... this is my moment."
You sat down. You opened your phone. You took a sip of coffee that was almost warm, and that's exactly when your internal parenting radar should have gone off.

Because in this house, quiet is never good. Quiet means something is being unwrapped, dumped, flushed, or "cooked."
You froze. Coffee halfway to your mouth, ears straining. Still no sound. That's when the dread set in. You stood up slowly, like in a horror movie, and tiptoed toward the void.

One child stood in the hallway with yogurt-covered hands and a suspiciously blank expression. Another had turned their toy kitchen into a full-scale chemistry lab, complete with every bottle of shampoo, lotion, bubble bath, and conditioner they could find in the bathroom cupboards. The sink was bubbling. The plastic fridge was smeared. A rubber duck floated in a foamy swirl of soap and body wash in their toy frying pan. The dog? Wet. And somehow smelling unmistakably like your husband's cologne.

You stood there blinking, trying to process it all. You let your guard down for sixty seconds—and the universe made sure you paid the price.

Check your quiet-time discoveries:
- ☐ Furniture has been "redecorated"
- ☐ Someone is now covered in something moist
- ☐ Someone made "art" on the walls
- ☐ You're not sure what they have in their hair, but it stinks
- ☐ The quiet was a trap, and you walked right into it

Fill in the blanks:
The suspicious silence lasted _____ minutes.
When I found them, they were _____.

Fill in any bubble that matches your emotional response right now:
- ○ Laugh and cry simultaneously
- ○ Yell, then feel guilty
- ○ Take a photo and send to your group chat with a weird name
- ○ Say nothing. Just walk away

Write your new parenting motto: "When it's quiet, it means _____."

Set a 1-minute timer and describe the most unhinged thing you have stumbled in on when your kids went silent:

_____
_____
_____
_____
_____
_____
_____
_____

Beware the Silence BINGO
What have you walked in on when they went quiet?

Mysterious smear	Something is wet	Items stacked dangerously	Object where it should NOT be	"He did it!" before you asked anything
Floor now textured	Sudden distinct smell	Fecal Scent	Drawer completely emptied	"Surprise" you didn't ask for
Self given makeover	Appliance messed with	FREE	Hair was cut	Trail of mess leading to kids
Something overflowed	A child scaled a high object	Suspicious stickiness	Child hiding and giggling	Something is taped to something else
New pile of something	Kitchen Utensils relocated	Wall was used as a canvas	Something flushed (possibly important)	Found naked

Today's Journaling Prompt: Things I Didn't Say Out Loud - Because "I'm fine" was a lie and everyone knows it.

You've probably already given your partner the daily recap: the basic timeline of meltdowns, messes, and mild miracles. But this page isn't for the curated version. This is for everything you wanted to say but didn't—because you were too tired, too polite, or too close to snapping and didn't want to risk jail time.

This is your emotional overflow drawer. The things you swallowed. The commentary you edited. The rage you dressed up as a sigh.

Let it out. You don't even have to use full sentences. Just get it down.

_____
_____
_____
_____
_____
_____
_____
_____
_____
_____
_____
_____
_____
_____
_____
_____
_____
_____
_____
_____
_____

Something tells me that today wine just wont cut it.
Therefore, I have not only a drink pairing for the absolute bullshit that was this day, but I included a cocktail recipe!

Disaster Daiquiri
For when the silence is suspicious and the Sharpie is permanent. You walked in. You saw it. They froze. You made eye contact. They said, "I can explain." But you said nothing because you were too busy calculating how much it's going to cost to fix this. You back out of the room, deciding the best course of action is to just let it happen and make a drink.

Ingredients:
2 oz white rum
1 oz fresh lime juice (for the sharp slap of reality)
¾ oz simple syrup
Ice

Instructions:
Shake all ingredients with ice like you're trying to physically beat the stress out of your day.
Strain into a glass.
Garnish with a lime wedge

The Disaster Daiquiri is deceptively sweet, simple, and slightly unhinged—just like your child when they "made you a surprise" and now the dog is missing fur.

Pairs well with:
– That moment you realize the glue was superglue
– Any sentence that begins with "I was just trying to…" .

Day 15
Snack Diplomacy

You offer a snack. Something simple, like apple slices or a handful of crackers.
They ask what else you have.
You mention yogurt.
They grumble.
You offer a granola bar.
They ask if it's the kind with chocolate chips or "the boring kind."
You hand them one. They stare at it for a moment and ask if they can have something after that too.
Eventually, they ask for cookies.
You say yes, but just one.
Suddenly it's an intense discussion.
"Can I have two?"
"How big is it?"
"What if I'm still hungry after?"
"Can I at least see how many are in the package?"
"Mine is smaller than his!"

You're not being unreasonable. You're just tired. You're also aware that you've had this exact interaction roughly 1,477,848,573,228,385.78 times this month alone.

You hand over the cookies, remind them dinner is coming soon, and start mentally prepping for round two. You already know they won't be hungry for dinner, but you are exhausted, not just from chasing them around all day, but mentally tired from the diplomat-level negotiations that just never stop. In your house, snack time is never really over.

Cognitive Reset: Reframing the Snack Spiral

Interrupt negative self-talk, guilt, or frustration around everyday decision-making—like giving your kid a second snack even though dinner's in 40 minutes.

Step 1: Identify the Thought

What's running through your head right now?
Examples might include:
– "I should be handling this better."
– "I gave in again—I'm too soft."
– "Why is this always a battle?"
Write yours here:

_____

_____

Step 2: Check the Reality

Answer honestly:
☐ Did I feed my child something?
☐ Did I offer reasonable choices?
☐ Did I try to keep it healthy or at least not ridiculous?
☐ Am I allowed to be tired of negotiating over cookies and crackers?

If you checked even one box, you're not failing, you're parenting.

Step 3: Re-frame the Thought

Take the thought you wrote in Step 1 and rewrite it in a more fair and balanced way.
Examples:
– "I'm not too soft. I'm choosing calm over a meltdown."
– "It's okay to be tired. I'm still doing the job."
– "One extra snack isn't a moral failure."
Now write yours:

_____

_____

Step 4: Pick a Grounding Phrase

Choose one to repeat in your head next time snack stress creeps in:

☐ "This isn't forever. It's just today."
☐ "Meeting needs isn't giving in."
☐ "I'm allowed to keep it simple."
☐ "Feeding a child doesn't need to be a debate."
☐ Write your own: _____

Mini Assignment:

Tonight, if you gave a snack and felt weird about it, don't overthink it. Instead, take a moment to recognize that you're showing up, and that's more than enough.

Serious time is over now, so let's talk about how the kids responded:

Check all that apply:

☐ Refused fruit like it was poison
☐ Cried over the size of the cookie
☐ Smeared what they didn't want into the placemat
☐ Used snack as currency to negotiate with a sibling for more
☐ Demanded "second lunch" or "pre-dinner"
☐ Meltdown over the food options
☐ Snuck around and took more of what they wanted without permission

What is the weirdest snack your kid has demanded?
_____

Fill in the blanks to write today's snack tale:
Today, my child ate a _____ (adjective) sandwich made of _____ (food) and _____ (random non-food item). He called it "The Ultimate _____ (emotion) Surprise."

You have been hassled 12 times today about snacks, so its time to give Mama her snack: *Sauvignon Blanc* is bright, sharp, and refreshingly honest. Basically, the mom version of "No, you may not have cookies right before dinner." This is the wine for the mom who's spent the afternoon negotiating over apples vs. crackers like it's a hostage situation. You offered good options, reasonable options, you said no five times, then yes once, then "fine, but sit at the table." You are snack-weary and emotionally full—and not in a good way.

Sauvignon Blanc tastes like diplomacy, not defeat. Tasting notes include:
– Zesty citrus
– Herbal undertones
– A hint of "I just need everyone to stop fucking talking for five minutes"

Sauvignon Blanc is best served cold, preferably while hiding behind the fridge door pretending to look for the sliced watermelon from last night that you already know is gone.
It pairs beautifully with:
– That one corner of the kitchen you try to keep clean
– A handful of stale crackers left on your kid's plate
– The moment your child says, "I'm still hungry," right after you finish cleaning up

Reward yourself with a glass of Sauvignon Blanc because sometimes, feeding tiny humans all day deserves more than applause. It deserves wine.

Let's not pretend. You didn't make yourself a meal today. You grazed. You hovered. You ate what was left. Because parenting is exhausting, your toddler declared war on spaghetti, and honestly? That cold chicken nugget was right there. This is your space to confess what you've consumed in the wild. No judgment. Just documentation. This is self-awareness. This is survival. This is motherhood. Describe the scraps you ate this week here:

_____
_____
_____
_____
_____
_____
_____
_____
_____
_____
_____
_____
_____
_____
_____
_____
_____
_____
_____
_____
_____
_____
_____
_____
_____
_____
_____

Day 16
Beauty School Dropout

It started quiet — that should've been your warning.
You were changing laundry, answering a work message, or — foolishly—peeing alone for thirty seconds, and in that small, sacred window, your child found the scissors.

Not the kid-safe ones, the sharp ones, the real ones.
By the time you saw the damage, it was too late. Hair, soft, beautiful toddler curls, were scattered across the bathroom floor. In the sink. On the dog. And standing proudly in the middle of it all? Your child. Smiling. Triumphant.

They had "given themselves a haircut."
Specifically, they'd removed a large patch of their perfect, curly locks from the the middle of their head, leaving behind an uneven crater of bold, chaotic self-expression. Not bangs. Not a trim. Just... creative liberty taken too far.

And of course, they asked, "Do you like it?"
Because what else would they ask after removing all evidence of your once-normal morning?

You told yourself, "Hair grows back," as your eyes burned with tears. You were planning to cut his hair soon, but this was your last baby and you wanted those baby-soft ringlets to last forever. Also burning in your eyes was the realization that nothing in parenting is truly safe, not even your scissor drawer.

Fill in the blanks:
The moment I saw his hair, I _____.
I tried to fix it by _____.
My internal monologue: " _____."

Fill in all bubbles that apply to a situation you have faced:
○ A salon emergency visit happened within the hour
○ Decided to "let it grow out and forget"
○ Gave everyone matching trims for solidarity
○ Called Grandma and let her deal with it
○ Took a photo and made it the Christmas card

Creative Writing Prompt: *Poetic Justice*
Write a short poem titled "Ode to the Missing Hair" (Feel free to rhyme, or don't—this is survival writing.)

Example:
My hair was here, and now it's not,
It vanished fast, a daring plot.
A patch is gone, I see the floor,
I might just shave and start once more.

Your turn:
Title: _____
Opening Line: _____
Middle Drama: _____
Emotional Ending: _____

Draw your kid's haircut.
Now draw the pile of hair you found.
That's it. That's the prompt.
Soon, there will be alcohol.

The hair one hurt, didn't it? I know. Here are some free lines for you to journal. Get it all out. *Put it in the book.*

Malbec—Because You Didn't Scream (Out Loud)

If you managed to look your child in the eye and not yell, "WHAT DID YOU DO?!"—go ahead and pour yourself a glass of Malbec. Malbec is rich, dark, and full of the kind of emotional depth usually reserved for therapy or emergency chocolate. It's what you drink when you've gone full dead-behind-the-eyes but still manage to say, "Wow, buddy... so creative!"

It pairs beautifully with:

– Nervous laughter
– Uneven toddler buzz cuts
– A passive-aggressive text to your partner saying, "Everything is fine... probably."
– The faint sound of clippers buzzing in the distance

Serve at room temperature, ideally while hiding in the bathroom your child just redecorated with his hair

Day 17
Daily Soundtrack

You woke up to the sound of someone yelling "MOM!" from across the house. Not because of an emergency, but because someone needed help finding a toy that was right in front of them.
That was your morning overture.

From there, the daily playlist grew:
– A sibling argument over who gets the blue silicone cereal bowl
– A dramatic reenactment of a favorite video game scene at full volume
– The noisiest toy you secretly threw out somehow made its way back, battery-powered and possessed
– And the constant hum of the latest YouTube song sensation which is now etched into your DNA

You haven't heard silence since 2018. You're starting to believe quiet might be a myth, like unicorns or going to the bathroom without an audience.

At some point, someone began humming the same six-note song over and over. You asked them to stop. They said, "I'm not even humming!" and then did it louder.

Even the fridge is beeping at you now.

By noon, you're googling "kid-free vacation packages" and wondering if grandma is available to take two kids. By dinner, your eyelid is twitching. The noisiest toy you definitely threw out somehow made its way back, battery-powered and possessed.

You love your kids, but you're one high-pitched jingle away from an emotional implosion. Overstimulated is a diplomatic way to explain this feeling. There is no end in sight.

Describe in three words today's loudest moment:

The most unbearable sound was:

A sound I'm still hearing even though it stopped hours ago:

If my house had a theme song today, it would be called:

Fill in all applicable bubbles: How did you attempt to manage the chaos? (And these for additional stress management: ○○○○○)
○ Hid the toy (again), this time under the couch
○ Turned on the vacuum just to drown them out
○ Screamed into a throw pillow
○ Put on your playlist just to feel human again
○ Joined in. Because if you can't beat them...
○ Became a raging lunatic and Incredible-Hulked the toy in half before dramatically tossing it in the trash. Bonus if you made your kids cry

Create Your Own Album:

Design your parenting playlist. Give each track a title that reflects your day:

_____ (Ex: "Screaming in Harmony")

_____ (Ex: "Snack Time Shouting Match")

_____ (Ex: "I Said Stop Hitting")

_____ (Ex: "Mysterious Thump Upstairs")

_____ (Ex: "I DON'T KNOW WHERE YOUR SHOE IS")

Alright Mama, this is hands-down the part of this book I am the most excited about. We are going to write a rap song and sing it together. I want to see my TikTok tagged with you performing this masterpiece. Buckle up, let's go. (@clara.harper.author)

[Intro — spoken]
Yo. This one goes out to all the moms out there…
Trying to whisper when they wanna scream.
Trying to breathe deep when someone just flushed their underwear.

(Verse 1)
It's 7 a.m. and I'm already _____ [emotion]
Someone's yelling about a missing _____ [household item], no one's listening
I step on a _____ [small painful object], drop my toast, now I'm limpin'
And I swear I just heard someone say, "_____ [absurd child request]"
Tryna keep my voice soft like a mindful queen
But inside I'm a volcano filled with _____ [explosive substance] and caffeine
"Use your words," I say with fake Zen flair
While one kid screams and the other one _____ [verb ending in -ed] a chair

(Chorus)
I'm gentle on the edge, got a smile that twitches
Prayin' my neighbor don't call CPS on these bitches
"Use an I-statement," I say through a grin
While I visualize launching a _____ [kitchen utensil] into the wind

(Verse 2)
Deep breaths, I say, in through the _____ [body part], out through the soul
While they argue over who gets the blue _____ [random item] bowl
I'm overstimulated, like a feral raccoon
In a Target on fire, under a full moon
Someone's humming, someone's shrieking,
I'm in the bathroom just _____ [verb ending in -ing] and leaking
My inner child's curled up with a blanket and wine
While my outer self says, "Let's use calm words this time!"

(Chorus)
I'm gentle on the edge, whisperin' like I'm fine
While they turn the living room into a toddler crime shrine
Counting backwards, holding space
While I mentally erase this entire damn place

(Bridge — spoken)
"Sweetie, I hear that you're upset.
But if you shriek in my face again while holding a raw egg,
I will lose my ever-loving _____ [four-letter word substitute]."

(Outro)
So here's to the moms stayin' soft while feelin' rage
Using therapy words on a post-apocalyptic stage
I'm calm. I'm chill. My eye just twitched.
But I haven't screamed yet, and that's my win... BITCH!

I know. That was awesome. We kicked ass. Suck a dick PTA Susan.

If motherhood were a mixtape, you'd be platinum by now.

You've narrated your entire day like a hostage negotiator and hype-woman rolled into one. You've got rhymes about missing shoes, endless cooking, emotional breakdowns, and wiping butts while answering work emails.

Today's assignment? Write the unreleased verses of your Mom Life Rap. Go full freestyle or just list the chaotic rhymes you've earned the right to drop. This isn't for the radio. This is for your own survival.

Gin & Tonic – Because your day had too many sound effects and not enough boundaries.

There comes a time—usually right after the fifth round of "Mom! MOM! MOOOOOM!"—when wine just won't cut it. Enter the classic Gin & Tonic. A drink so crisp, so calming, so refreshingly adult... it almost makes you forget the mystery clanging coming from upstairs. You don't care that it is a grandma drink, you wish you were a grandma because that would mean you got to enjoy kids in doses, giving them back when you've had enough.

This cocktail pairs beautifully with:
– Shutting the bathroom door and pretending you can't hear them
– Whispering "shhh" to no one in particular
– That haunted stare you get after hearing a toy sing "la la la" for 6 straight hours
– Fantasizing about converting the garage into a recording studio

Day 18
The One About Tantrums

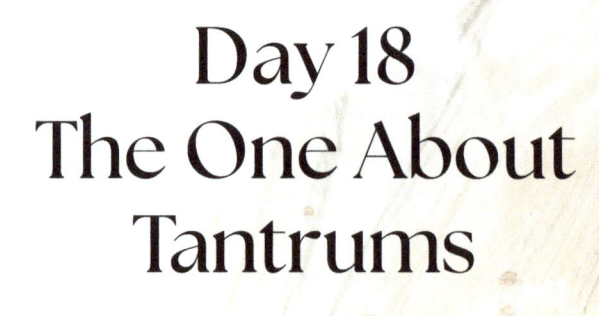

You thought it would be a quick trip. One stop. Just milk. Maybe some bread and cereal, nothing dramatic, but now you're in aisle 7 holding a dented can of spaghetti hoops like it's a white flag, trying to negotiate with a child mid-meltdown because the cereal box is "wrong." Not expired. Not torn. Just wrong because it doesn't have the dinosaur on it.

Not just a dinosaur—*the* dinosaur. The green one. From the commercial. With sunglasses. Obviously, that's critical to his argument. You're sweating through your bra, and wonder if your boob sweat will be visible from the outside at any moment.

You're trying to stay calm while your child sobs, fists clenched, this is his Alamo. Meanwhile, your other child is... gone. You already had to ask store employees for help once today because he somehow climbed into the dairy fridge—into it—and slipped through the back panel like it was a portal to Narnia. You found him waving from the stockroom like he worked there. They were nice about it. Too nice. You're pretty sure someone followed you after that... just in case.

Now you've burned through your purse snacks. That last emergency granola bar is melted into the lining of your bag and stuck to a receipt from 2019. A stranger just looked at you with the exact mix of judgment and pity you've trained yourself to ignore. You still have half of your list to finish.

You haven't even made it to checkout, where the real hell begins: the wall of candy, cheap plastic toys, and that inevitable question: "Can I have it?" You'll say no. Then yes. Then hate yourself for it. Someone has already lost a shoe. You're trying not to lose your will to live with it. Send help. Or snacks. Or just open the wine aisle and look the other way.

Write a fake customer review of your outing today:

_____
_____
_____

Role Play Rewrite: If your child were the store manager, how would they handle tantrums?

_____
_____
_____

1. Grocery Store Breakdown Report
Official Incident Form #CART-22
Please complete the following fields for emotional processing and/or evidence in case of future lawsuits (or therapy).

Date of Incident: _____
Time Elapsed Before Regret Set In: _____ minutes
Number of Children Present: _____
Estimated Decibel Level of Meltdown:
☐ Moderate
☐ Alarming
☐ Glass-shattering
☐ Internal screaming only

Most chaotic moment occurred in the _____ aisle, when

_____
_____
_____
_____

Store employee involvement:
- ☐ Nodded silently
- ☐ Helped retrieve a runaway child
- ☐ Witnessed it all and backed away slowly
- ☐ Said "You're doing amazing" (they were lying)

Your coping mechanism included:
- ☐ Whispering to yourself "we're almost done" 47 times
- ☐ Bribery
- ☐ Wild, empty threats
- ☐ Purchasing unnecessary _____ to make it stop

Final damage:
Lost item: _____
Emotional toll: _____
Purchased out of desperate need to de-escalate: _____

Follow-up plan:
- ☐ Never return
- ☐ Send partner next time
- ☐ Order groceries online forever
- ☐ Day drinking

Because someone lost their mind today—and it might've been you... Tantrums are loud, they're dramatic, they're unpredictable, and somehow, they always happen in public near breakable objects or during the exact moment you finally sat down.

This page is for processing the emotional storm: theirs, yours, all of it. You don't need solutions—just space to unpack it.
Describe that memorable banger, you know the one. The tantrum that still makes your eyes bulge and blood pressure rise when you think about it.

You survived the errand. The noise. The stares. The meltdown over something confusing and completely non-negotiable. You made it out with some of what you came for, a little bit of your dignity intact, and zero emotional snacks left in your mental pantry. You may have lost a kid for a few minutes, but at least you can rest assured that no one would want to kidnap that asshole anyway.

That doesn't call for applause.
That calls for tequila. Immediately!

Enter: The *Palóma*. Let's get into the details.
Light. Refreshing. Slightly salty.
Just like your mood.

Ingredients:
2 oz tequila (or whatever splash feels right today)
2 oz fresh grapefruit juice
1/2 oz lime juice
2 oz sparkling water
Pinch of salt
Ice
Optional: sugar or salt rim
Instructions:
Pour everything into a cocktail shaker and shake it baby!.

Pairs best with:
– Chips and salsa eaten on the bathroom toilet with the door locked so they can't find you.

You survived. You earned it. Let the citrus cleanse your soul.

Day 19
PTA Susan's Pinterest Board

It all started with a post. There she was again. PTA Susan. Glowing like a smug suburban deity with her curated kitchen and hand-lettered chalkboard menu, casually posting "a fun lil' Fall craft to do with your kiddos this weekend!" It was a paper leaf garland. It looked easy. It looked cute. It looked achievable. You were delusional.

Fueled by coffee and a deep need to prove you are also fun and capable, you gathered supplies: construction paper, glue, markers, string, scissors with the squiggly edge. You even lit a pumpkin scented candle because you are nothing if not committed to the vibe. Your toddler lasted four minutes. Just long enough to scribble on one leaf and start eating the glue stick—not even the cap, just aggressively biting the glue like it was string cheese. Your older one tried, he really did, but got distracted halfway through and began punching holes in everything he could reach with the hole puncher: leaves, your grocery list, one sleeve of his shirt. You looked away for a literal second, and in that time, the glitter container was opened. Fully. It is now part of your home's permanent texture.

The scissors—which you had definitely put out of reach—were now firmly in the hands of your two-year-old, who was aiming them vaguely toward the table... and then toward the dog. The dog, by the way, is now missing a small patch of fur and is sparkling like a craft store exploded around him. You don't remember what happened after that. Your gentle parenting voice left your body. It packed a small bag, waved goodbye, and whispered, "You're on your own now, bitch."

In its place rose something ancient. Something feral. You blacked out for a second and when you came to, you were ranting about "real glue", and "why we don't use glitter in this godforsaken house."

Check all that happened during your "fun activity" moment:
- ☐ Someone lost interest before you even got the supplies out
- ☐ You did 99.99999 % of the work
- ☐ The "easy" instructions turned into a full-on hostage situation
- ☐ Your child asked, "Are we done yet?" before the glue dried
- ☐ You found scissors where scissors should not be
- ☐ Both kids melted down and you yelled "WE ARE HAVING FUN, GODDAMMIT!"
- ☐ The table was covered in glue, glitter, and one mystery smear
- ☐ Your child's only contribution was crying and making a mess
- ☐ You started muttering to yourself and haven't stopped since

The project lasted:
- ☐ Under 5 minutes
- ☐ Long enough for you to regret everything
- ☐ An hour, but only because cleanup took 45 minutes

My favorite part of the craft was:
_____

The moment I knew it was over was when:
_____

The one item I'll be finding pieces of for the next 6 months:
_____

Emotional Processing Debrief: A Craft-Time Cognitive Collapse

"What the actual hell is wrong with us?"
Try this reframe:
"This wasn't a craft. It was a slow-motion breakdown with scissors."
Now your turn:
When I saw the mess, I thought:
"_____"
(Example: "Should I clean this or just set it on fire?")
A more helpful perspective might be:
"_____"
(Example: "At least no one cut their own hair this time.")

Next time, I'll try:
☐ Choosing an activity that doesn't involve glue, glitter, or emotional risk
☐ Accepting that "fun" is a scam invented by people with off-screen nannies
☐ Pretending whatever happened was intentional "process art"
☐ Quietly deleting the original idea from my brain and from Susan's feed

Craft Project for mom: A Visual Exercise in Processing Suburban Perfection Pressure

Today's craft is a therapeutic masterpiece disguised as paper art. Start with construction paper and cut out a vaguely human shape. Label her "PTA Susan." Give her a signature messy bun using yarn or shredded tissues, and glue on giant fake lashes that complement her giant fake boobs. Sculpt her chest out of crumpled foil or two giant cotton balls. Add a stretchy "Get Ready With Me" TikTok video headband using string, elastic, or a hair tie that's lost its will to live. Erase any lines on her Botox saturated forehead and overfilled lips with whatever marker still works. Around her, paste little captions cut out of magazines like a serial killer with sayings like: "Is that gluten free?" and "my kids didn't have screen time until they were seven," and "my 8 year old prefers breastmilk." This is not petty. This is preventative medicine.

Drink Reward: The *"Why Did I Think This Would Be Fun" Fizz*
Ingredients:
– 3 oz of whatever sparkling wine you already opened earlier this week
– A splash of the juice box your kid left half-finished on the table
– Ice from the freezer that smells a little like chicken nuggets
– Stir with the back end of a fork because all your spoons are in the sink
– Serve in a coffee mug, because it's the only thing that's clean

Pairs well with:
– Half-finished crafts still stuck to the table
– Dried glue under your fingernails
Toast to yourself:
"I gave them a memory. I also gave up halfway through. Both are valid."

This is the official page where you will glue your Paper Voodoo Doll of PTA Susan. As you glue her to the page, think fondly about the rage you felt watching her latest reel about the animal shapes she cut out of fruit for her kid's breakfast bento boxes. Dwell on how she casually mentions her 4 AM workouts and says things like "we all have the same 24 hours in the day!" Do not worry. This is not dark magic. It's arts and crafts for the emotionally unstable. It's called *therapy*. Please, *please* tag this author on Tiktok and present your masterpiece to the world! (@clara.harper.author)

Day 20
The Social Event Spiral

You said yes to the birthday invite. A girl from Kindergarten. Her mom seemed nice in the hallway. How bad could it be? Then you pulled up to the house and instantly knew. This wasn't a bounce-house-in-the-yard party. This was *intentional beige*. Designer doormat. Matching planters. A chalkboard sign on an easel that said "Welcome to Emerson's Magical Five!" in hand-lettered cursive. Emerson. Of course her name is Emerson.

Inside, it was worse. Every wall was white, every decorative item was glass, and the house smelled like eucalyptus. And the food—dear God, the food. Bagels sliced into fourths with smoked salmon and dill, fruit skewers organized by color gradient, and tiny cups of hummus with baby carrots and parsley standing upright like mini gardens, and much more. The only kid friendly thing on the table were those little Oreo flower pots with candy worms.

Your son walked in, made direct eye contact with the mother, and said: "My pants are pinching my penis."

That was before you could even hang up your jacket. You fake-laughed. Emerson's mom paused for one beat too long. You whispered something about growth spurts and pulled him aside—but it was too late. The tone had been set. Then came the food table. While the other parents delicately plated food for their children, your child reached right for a tray of canapés, grabbed two without asking, shoved a fistful in his mouth, chewed twice, and yelled: "BLECH! What is this? It tastes *disgusting!*"

You saw Emerson's mom blink three times before she quietly excused herself to rearrange the napkins. You tried to recover. You offered to help. You made a comment about "how cute everything is" and "wow, I wish I had the talent." But you could feel it. You were *that* guest. The one who brought chaos in light-up sneakers and ketchup-stained khakis. Oh and you had massive pit stains.

Choose Your Exit Strategy:
- "He's on the verge of a feral outburst, and I'd rather it not happen near your nice things"
- "If we don't leave now, someone's getting naked or injured. Possibly both."
- "He's entering his danger nap window—if he sleeps five minutes in the car, bedtime is canceled"
- "He just made the face, and I'm not cleaning that up here"
- "I forgot to thaw dinner, and we've already had cereal twice this week"
- "We've reached our polite-in-public statute of limitations. We're on borrowed minutes now"
- "If I have to stop him from licking one more object, I'm going to scream"
- "Our emotional stability has entered sudden-death overtime"

Fill in the blanks:

The exact moment I knew it was over was when _____.

I tried to smooth it over by _____.

Emerson's mom said it was "no big deal," but her eyes said _____.

Post-Party Coping Scale:

How are you doing?
- Mostly fine. Just a little dead inside.
- Avoiding eye contact at school drop-off now.
- Googling how to change your last name.
- Emotionally curled into the fetal position in your car, eating drive-thru fries.

Tell me the single most embarrassing thing your child has done in public.

_____
_____
_____
_____
_____
_____
_____
_____
_____
_____

Drink Reward: *The Kindergarten Party Painkiller*
–2 oz rum (because this was a mental injury)
–1 oz pineapple juice
–Squeeze of orange
–Dash of coconut cream
–Shake and pour over ice, imagining you're somewhere no one is judging your parenting

Pairs well with:
–Deep-breathing while rage-folding laundry
–The cold sweat of remembering he said "penis" in a stranger's house

Day 21
The Last

You've made it to the final day. Barely. Not with grace, not with wisdom—just sheer momentum and whatever's left in your emotional gas tank after parenting on hard-mode for 21 straight days.

You're not even sure what finally wore you down today. It wasn't the whining, or the spilled juice, or the fourth request for a snack while dinner was literally in front of them. It was something smaller. Dumber. Maybe it was finding half a banana on the back of the toilet like it was just part of the décor. Maybe it was watching your child put a toy screw in his mouth, pulling it out, and saying, "Don't worry—I didn't swallow it *this* time."

Maybe it was the moment you realized you hadn't sat down once without someone immediately climbing on top of you.

You've said things no human should ever have to say out loud. You've narrated bodily functions, negotiated over sock choices, and explained—again—why we can't dry our wet socks in the microwave.

Your coffee is forever cold, your nerves are fried, and your kid just asked for another snack when you are literally plating lunch.

But here you are: tired, frazzled, and still showing up. Because that's what moms do.

So for today—the last day—we won't tell you to savor anything, or enjoy the little moments, or "cherish this time." You already know. You're just too damn tired to pretend it's beautiful all the time. This day is for you. The real you. The version that survived... and that's more than enough.

Fill in the Blank: Last Nerve Edition
Today I hit my breaking point when _____.
The most ridiculous thing I said out loud was:
"_____."
My child responded by _____.
I attempted to cope by _____,
but it only made things _____.
The moment I officially gave up was when _____.

Fill in the bubbles: Rate Your Final Form
Today, I feel like...
○ A deflated balloon with snack crumbs stuck to it
○ A slightly haunted version of my former self
○ Surprisingly calm, which is suspicious
○ One meltdown away from becoming a local news story
○ Just numb enough to call it peace
○ Emotionally held together by dry shampoo
○ Still standing, somehow

Write a Haiku: Ode to Survival
Traditional 5-7-5 syllable format.
Theme: your current mental state.
Example:

    Cold coffee again
    Tiny voices never stop
    I just wanted toast

Your turn:
Line 1: _____
Line 2: _____
Line 3: _____

The "Perfect" Parenting Day

Today, I woke up feeling _____ (adjective) and immediately stepped on a _____ (object).

I asked my child to _____ (verb) but instead they _____ (past tense verb) a _____ (food item) into the _____ (appliance). Then I found _____ (something wet) in a place where only _____ (emotion) should be.

Lunch was a delightful combination of _____ (plural noun) and _____ (random snack), followed by a bold tantrum about _____ (noun).

At bedtime, I told myself, "This is fine," while ___ _____ (verb ending in -ing) into a pile of _____ (emotion) and _____ (plural noun). _____ (favorite four-letter word starting with F and ending with K) my life.

What nearly broke you today?
_____
_____
_____

What held you together?
_____
_____
_____

What did you do that no one saw but deserves a damn medal?
_____
_____
_____

Take up the whole page. Vent. Brag. Spiral artistically. Or just draw a giant circle and write "NOPE" in it. This one's yours.
_____
_____
_____
_____
_____
_____
_____
_____
_____
_____
_____
_____
_____
_____

Being the last day of our 21-day journey, this one deserves not one but two celebratory drinks!

1. The *"We're Still Here" Sparkler*
Because no one died, and that's what we call success.
Ingredients:
– 3 oz sparkling wine (for the fizz you didn't feel today)
– 1 oz elderflower liqueur (to convince yourself you're classy)
– Splash of orange juice (or whatever juice your kid didn't finish)
– Ice, a straw, and no interruptions
Instructions:
Pour into the cleanest glass you can find (coffee mug is fine). Drink it standing up while pretending you don't hear "Moooom!"
Pairs well with:
Crumbs in your bra and dignity in shambles.

2. The *"Last Nerve Margarita"*
Made to honor the nerve you lost somewhere around snack #4.
Ingredients:
– 2 oz tequila (because wine won't cut it today)
– 1 oz lime juice (fresh or not—no judgment)
– 1 oz triple sec (or orange juice and chaotic energy)
– Salt rim (optional)
Instructions:
Shake with ice, pour into a glass rimmed with salt. Sip slowly while staring into the void and muttering "we made it."

Pairs well with:
Resentful silence and someone yelling from the bathroom.

I never told anyone this, but... Tell me something about yourself that is so scandalous that I can't stop thinking about it for days. Don't forget to share on TikTok! (@clara.harper.author)

The end.

That's it. Go lie down.

To the Moms of Young Kids Everywhere,

Look at you. Still here. Still fucking functioning. (Debatable, but we're calling it a win.) You've wiped noses with your own sleeve. You've held someone's sticky hand while peeing. You've eaten dinner standing up, answered questions mid-shower, and considered faking appendicitis just to get some rest. You have whispered "what the actual hell" more times than you can count and still managed to show up for the people who depend on you with the strength of a thousand fruit-snack-fueled warriors. We see you.

You are not the serene, linen-wearing mom from the Instagram ads. You are the mom who scraped yogurt off her bra at school drop-off and called it clean. The mom who lovingly packed a lunch and then forgot to put it in the backpack. The mom who has Googled "how much screen time is too much" and then hit play anyway. And guess what? You're doing it. Not perfectly. Not quietly. But relentlessly.

You are the bedtime negotiator, the emotional barometer, the snack curator, and the crisis containment unit. You have learned to function in conditions that would make Navy SEALs cry. You have held it together with Cocomelon playing in the background and a child screaming because the toast is "cut wrong."
This workbook? It's ending. But your chaos? Oh honey, that's eternal.

Still — something in you has changed. You've found humor in the mess, solidarity in the struggle, and maybe, just maybe, a little grace for yourself along the way. So here's your permission slip to not savor every moment, to scream into a pillow, to hide in the pantry, to throw a fruit snack pack at a child and call it a peace offering, to do the bare minimum and still count it as success, because if your kid is alive, fed (ish), and moderately clothed, then guess what?
You've won.

You are a legend. A warrior. A wine-sipping, tear-wiping, chaos-carrying queen. So go forth. Collapse on the couch. Eat the hidden chocolate. Ignore the laundry. And never, ever forget: You are not alone. You are not failing. You are just parenting tiny humans who think band-aids fix everything and that time is a lie. You've got this. Kind of. That's enough.

With love,
Your Fellow Burnt-Out Mom in the Trenches

Clara Harper

Certificate
of survival

This Certificate
is Presented To

_____

_____ has completed 21 consecutive days of domestic combat, emotional management, and footwear retrieval under extreme conditions.
She has withstood:
- Multiple screaming fits, none of which were her own (almost)
- Questionable substances on household surfaces
- Repetitive snack-based negotiations that went absolutely nowhere
- Conversations that started with "Guess what I put in my mouth"
- And the sheer psychological toll of trying to pee without an audience

Despite being under-caffeinated, over-touched, and emotionally ambushed before 8 a.m., she persisted.
She did not rise above.
She did not grow stronger.
She simply refused to go down with the ship.
And that, frankly, is enough.
Awarded on this day: _____

May your coffee be hot, your socks be matching, and your children forget how to find you when you're hiding in the bathroom.

About the Author

Clara Harper is a children's book author, mother, wine enthusiast, and expert in pretending everything is fine. She lives in Germany with her husband and two sons, who serve as the primary source of her content, emotional damage, and unmatched comedic material.

Clara began writing children's books when she couldn't find quality stories to help her own kids navigate big feelings. That quickly evolved into a full-blown career in emotional monster taming and sarcasm therapy—especially for moms who are barely holding it together but still showing up.

When she's not wrangling children or writing emotionally unstable workbooks, Clara runs Published Nerd LLC, and can usually be found hiding in the laundry room with a glass of red and a notebook full of passive-aggressive parenting ideas.

Want more monsters, meltdowns, and relatable mom content?

Scan the QR code below to visit: www.claraharperbooks.com and subscribe to her blog. While there, take a look at her other books.

www.ingramcontent.com/pod-product-compliance
Lightning Source LLC
Chambersburg PA
CBHW042334150426
43194CB00005B/154